One to Sing, One to Haul

A Gordon Bok Collection

TIMBERHEAD
Camden, Maine

Woodcarvings and drawings by Gordon Bok

For permission to record or copy any works contained herein, please
contact Timberhead Music, PO Box 840, Camden, Maine 04843
or email: info@gordonbok.com.

ISBN 1-879622-02-5

First Edition
Printed in the United States of America

Contents

4   *Introduction*
5   *Preface*
7   *A Note about the Instruments and the Music*

8   All My Sailors
10   The Bird Rock
12   Matinicus
16   Shipyard Boat
17   The Gift
18   Dark Old Waters
19   Captain Dave's Delight
20   Boat of Silver
21   Culebra
26   Dear Old Vessels (One for the *Taber*)
28   Bay Saint Mary
30   Against the Moon
31   Archie Take Your Boots Off / Namagati (Northwest Airt)
32   Another Bay
34   Chall Eilibh
35   Good Wish
36   Janko (Yanka)
37   Gordon's Farewell
38   Harbors of Home
39   Gordon's Fancy
40   The Wreck of the Schooner *Ellen Munn*
42   The Ledge-End of the Fiddler
44   Long Life to the Moon
45   Rory Dall
46   The Sea Wife
48   Boats of Peter's River
50   Fiddler of Dooney
52   Harp Song of the Dane Women
54   The Shepherd's Call
56   Loni
58   Morag
60   Carmina Gadelica

61   Mussels in the Corner
62   Wild Birds
66   Wiscasset Schooners
68   Karl Edstrom and the *Hesper*
70   Woodworker's Litany (Season to Season)
72   Jericho (Ho-ro, the Wind and Snow)
74   Beaches of Lucannon
76   Blackbird
78   The Ways of Man
80   The Schooner *Ellenmore*
82   *Liza Jane*
84   Old Fat Boat (Mattapoisett Harbor Inventory)
88   Sally
90   Safe
91   Lily o' the North
92   McKeon's Coming
93   'Poem' for Jerry Rasmussen
94   Hearth and Fire
96   Schooner *Fred Dunbar*
98   Bok and the Moon
99   You Who Have Found Your Face
100   Pearly
106   Thumpy
110   Turning of the Year
111   The Kind Land (Serinam)
112   Entrained Water

113   *Jan Harmon*
114   *J. B. Goodenough*
115   *Title/Album Locator*
116   *Index*

Introduction

It's been more than 20 years since my first book of songs was published, and I've had quite a few hints that another one might be welcome. But where to start? I've learned, cobbled together and created a lot of music—with a lot of people—in that time.

After long consultation with my advisors (family and friends) we decided to start with this book. It consists mostly of things I've recorded: mostly solos, both traditional and contemporary music, a lot of pieces of my own making and some by others I've met along the way that you wouldn't easily find elsewhere. For now we'll leave the cantefables, oratorios and other choral pieces, instrumental duets, trios and quartets, musical plays and whatall, for later books.

Jane Kerrigan originally started this project with me. Our community was deeply saddened by her death. Matt Szostak took over after we lost Jane.

I want to thank Matt for initial search and organizing, Ken Gross for graphic design, photography, layout and creative thinking, John Roberts for transcriptions and advice, Carol Rohl for proofreading and title search, Glenn Jenks for final music proof, and to Team Kallet/Blodgett, Anne Dodson, and Paul Sullivan (and all of the above), for help, support and advice (both helpful and hilarious) through the years.

And thanks to Lois Lyman for taking on the job of keeping the whole project organized and moving, and to Selkie O'Mira for seeing it through to the printer. It must have felt like shifting Lake Champlain with a pitchfork, most days.

I'm also grateful to all you songmakers who have loaned me your work over the years—surely a risky business. Bless you.

And it should never go without saying, to all you who have supported my work over the years: thank you for your patience and faith.

Gordon Bok
Camden, Maine

Preface

Many years ago I was studying music at Yale. Like all music students, I pored and pondered for years over the vast treasure trove of musical scores in the library. I examined the architecture of Beethoven sonatas, the bittersweet melodies of Chopin and the indescribable orchestrations of Maurice Ravel. It was a thrilling and heady time, and I began to feel that all the music worth knowing about lay before me in those silent stacks, just waiting for me to open the pages.

By a lucky chance I visited a friend's room one evening and my musical world changed forever. My friend was listening to *A Tune For November* by Gordon Bok. As I fell under the spell, I realized that this was a whole new region of music, full of deep beauty and life and subtlety which I had never imagined before. It rocked and rolled and swayed and swung and comforted me. And it had an exciting fragrance of brine in it which I had never experienced in the close, bookish atmosphere of the library stacks. It was as though someone had taken my map of the musical universe and unfolded a whole panel that I hadn't known was there. From then on I have never tired of the music of Gordon Bok. It has continued to sing to my soul long after many of those scores I studied have been forever put aside. That's why it is a landmark honor for me to say a few words about this lovely book.

When you think about it, a songbook is an extraordinary thing. It's an invitation to a party and the map for how to get there. It's a magician inviting you backstage to show you how he does a few of his tricks, and showing you how to do them too. It's a peek behind the veil, an explanation of the blueprints. It's a place at the banquet table. And with this songbook, Gordon Bok invites you to sit next to him at the feast.

Songbooks may even be a somewhat endangered species. Once they were the only way, other than a live performance, in which a composer could share his or her musical ideas with anyone. But now, of course, we share our music through audio technology, so that in the twinkling of a few electrons, an adventurous listener in rural China can hear the magical sound of Gordon Bok himself, in all its gorgeous richness. So writing a songbook has changed from being a labor of necessity to an act of generosity. In an era when you're lucky if a DJ announces the name of a song, it's rare indeed to be able to see the notes of the melody, the lyrics, the chords and even the guitar tablature, all offered to you as an invitation to make the music your own, and to share in the joy of playing it yourself. And when, as in the book you're now holding, the songs are also embellished with personal commentaries and reflections by the composer, as well as his lovely and loving artwork, well, this is an extraordinary songbook indeed.

Of course, not all songs are well suited for life in a songbook. Some are too fragile, some are too complex. Others can only live in the rarified atmosphere of a digital recording studio. These kinds of songs can't survive the transformations that a songbook song has to undergo. They'd crumble when you tried to unwrap them. They seem to carry an unspoken but firm warning: "Don't try this at home."

Gordon Bok's songs are of an entirely different nature. Like Bach's music, Bok's music is sturdy. Durable. Gordon's songs are handcrafted out of water and wind, wood, wire and words. And as a result, they can be handled, turned over, tried out, re-created and transformed over and over again without any signs of wear. In fact, I've sometimes heard Gordon speak about "making" a song, and "putting a song together." It's the same terminology a Maine boatbuilder uses to describe the creation of a fine wooden yacht. And you can bet your life that Gordon's songs will take you on a journey just as glorious and rewarding as any windjammer.

So by all means, grab hold of this book. Take it home, and relax and enjoy the songs. Sing them, play them, transpose them, and make them your own. You won't hurt them a bit. They won't fall apart even with a little rough treatment. And, better yet, ten years from now, they'll still be fresh. Gordon's music has been in my soul for thirty years now, and it's still fresh. What's more, you'll find these songs are loyal friends. They will faithfully repay whatever effort and attention you lavish on them.

As for me, I guess my fondest hope for this book is that it will find its way into the stacks of every college library in the country. There it will sit, quiet and unassuming, patiently wafting it's tangy, sweet perfume into the musty air, until it attracts the attention of some bright-eyed, unsuspecting students. And then, for the sake of their educations, I can only hope that Gordon's music ambushes them the way it ambushed me.

Paul Sullivan
Blue Hill, Maine
September 10, 2000

A Note about the Instruments and the Music

I play a twelve-string guitar built by Nick Apollonio (Apollo Instruments) in Rockport, Maine. He and I developed this model over quite a few years; it has a longer-than-usual scale length, an extra-wide fingerboard to accommodate my fat finger-ends, a large body, and is tuned four half-steps below standard: at C instead of E. Usually I tune the bass course down a whole tone below that, so my "D"-chord is a B-flat. I use a capo on that instrument.

I also play a *laud* (la-ood), a small, teardrop-shaped instrument of Spanish lineage, which Nick built for me, also with an extra wide board. It has a shorter scale-length, and is tuned (in six unison pairs) like a regular steel-string guitar capoed at the third fret. This is an adaptation from a Portuguese/Spanish instrument.

The instrument I've played the longest is the nylon-strung six-string Spanish guitar, which I first began to learn from my mother and her sisters and brother. I have tried to be influenced by listening to recordings of such worthies as Laurindo Almeida, Andres Segovia, Josh White and Leadbelly, as well as students of mine who had studied classical and flamenco guitar, and friends like Peter Platenius who was raised in South America and introduced me to a lot of that music. My favorite Spanish guitars have been one built by Ronald Pinkham (Woodsound Studio in Rockland, Maine) in 1980 and my mother's old guitar, built before I was born in New York by R.A. Mango, and rebuilt in 1998 by Nick Apollonio. I don't use a capo on these guitars.

My most recent instrument is a small, slightly-modified (of course) viol da gamba, also built by Nick. It has 5 strings tuned at (cello) C, G, C, E, and (cello) A. It has inset Delrin frets instead of the usual string frets. I use a regular cello bow. I also play a 6-string "cellamba" (an old name for a cello that's been converted to a viol da gamba), built by David White of Albuquerque, NM, fretted and regraduated by Ron Pinkham. That one's tuned G (below cello C) D, G, C, E, A: pretty normal bass viol da gamba tuning.

I have developed a few other instruments, but these are the ones I play.

About the tablature

Many of these tunes we play with friends, using a variety of instruments including guitar, cellamba, laud, harp, flute, fiddle, and hammered dulcimer; so we have not included tablature for them. We have added tablature for those tunes that I always play on a guitar or laud. The tablature represents one way of playing a tune: not the way, nor perhaps exactly my own way of playing it; but it should come out sounding right. Feel free to make your own way.

You'll find the odd discrepancy in lyrics—the written music tends to follow the way I sing it, whereas the printed lyrics usually follow the author's original text.

All My Sailors

Sailing an old boat back to Maine in the summer of 1991, I was reminded of the many people who have helped me over the years. Not just the older friends who tried to give me their wisdom and the skills to stay alive, but all those others, too, whose company makes it so worth living.

Spanish guitar, recording in A.

The first boat I took out to sea, I didn't know where that boat was go-ing; All I want was a-way from here and all I knew was keep on row-ing.____ The first boat I put out to sea, I wouldn't have none to sail with me: none to row and none to tow, and none to stow this car-go down.____

A) The first boat I took out to sea
    I didn't know where that boat was going
    All I want was away from here
    And all I knew was keep on rowing

    B) The first boat I put out to sea
        I wouldn't have none to sail with me
        None to row and none to tow
        And none to stow this cargo down

A) But I come a-rolling through the calm
    And all my leading stars are gone
    There's three old sailors by my helm
    Tell me I don't sail alone

    B) One named Peter, one named Sol
        One don't claim no name at all
        One to sing and one to haul
        And one to heave me when I pawl[1]

    B) And when I stumble on the reef,
        I had three good sailors take my grief
        One to sail and one to bail
        And one to hear me when I wail

A) Now if the wind come staving more
    I won't need to run for shore[2]
    I don't need to reef and tack
    'Cause I don't need to bring her back

    B) Fog and foul or fair and free
        It's all the flaming same to me
        'Cause all the good hands ever sail
        Are rolling down my weather rail

A) And when I turn for making land
    I got three good sailors to my hand
    One to stay and one to pray
    And one to lay this anchor down

    B) And when I hoist my sail again
        Come in sun or go in rain
        All the sailors in the sea
        Come hand and haul and steer with me

        One to row and one to tow
        And one to ease me when I go[3]

—Ketch *Sionna* 1991

[1] pawl = rest (or perhaps "pall")
[2] sometimes "harbor"
[3] sometimes "heave" instead of ease

9

The Bird Rock

Molly Schauffler sang me a Norwegian song called "Måken" (The Seagull).
I took the idea and her translation and made this song from it, to my own
melody and cadence. The pictures are from the part of my childhood that
helped me choose the water as a place to work. I quote a scrap of the original
song in the last chorus, "Der hvor alle Måker er" — "There where all the
gulls are."

1.Row, my child, to the Bird Rock,____ where the gulls are sail - ing
2.Row, my child, be____ row - ing;____ for the day goes down be -

free._____ Dreams they do bring and dream - ing;_____
fore._____ And the ship of fair - ies sail - ing_____ to a

dreams of the cold green____ sea._____ And who would be there but
dark and a dis - tant____ shore._____ And who then could say what

you, love, to____ see what dreams there be?_____ Ho - ray, ho-
trea - sure would ever a - wait her there?_____

row, oh hoo - ro._____ *(last time)* Der hvor al - le må - ker er._____

(played)

©1983 Gordon Bok BMI

10

1.   Row, my child, to the bird rock, where the gulls are sailing free.
     Dreams they do bring and dreaming, dreams of the cold green sea;
     And who would be there but you, love, to see what dreams there be?
     (Ho-ray ho-row oh hoo-ro)

2.   Row, my child, be rowing: for the day goes down before
     And the ship of fairies sailing, to a dark and a distant shore
     And who then could say what treasure would ever await her there?

3.   Sing, my child, for the kingdom that ever we thought was gone,
     The ship-of-ghosts is sailing, and that one will always return.
     Drowned are the lands and gone the sails, and the gull is their voice alone.

4.   Row, my child, the day is fair where the young birds learn to sing.
     The sun is a wheel of wonder that only the gull can spin,
     And the gull is the low and lifting swell that the world has given wing.

After the last chorus: "Der hvor alle måker er"
(pronounced dahr voor alleh mauker ar.)

Inspired by the Norwegian song "Måken" (Gulls)
sung by Molly Schauffler, the Barred Islands, 1982.

Matinicus

Of the children I went to grade-school with in Camden, there were some I admired very much. We all scattered to the winds, of course, but I re-met one, Judy Bunker (nee Gerrish), when a schooner I was on put into Matinicus Island.

We talked a little: she'd married a fisherman there, had a wee baby, and was very happy.

A few years later I heard she had died of cancer, and I had been making a little, private lament tune for her, odd times. But then I met another Matinicus man fishing out of New Bedford at the time, and he told me how grateful he was, not only for knowing Judy, but for the gift of her two daughters, who gave off the same kind of light that she had.

So from the parts of the sad tune I made another, more like Judy herself, and play them both together to remind me that joy and grief are often made of the same ingredients.

Spanish guitar in D.

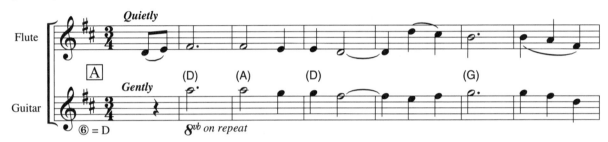

12

*Continue with varied 6/8 accompaniment, incorporating indicated notes

(ritard. on repeat)

D.S. al Fine

(Fine)

Shipyard Boat

Before she died they put a cabin on her and renamed her.
When I knew her she was only Susie,
name nor hail across her faded transom, a rangy,
halfdecked workboat—no cleats, just wooden bitts.

From my backporch bed against the dew-deep hill
chill with spruce and shaggy arborvitae,
I'd hear her long drone broadening the bay
in the halftide hush of dawn.
                                And I'd run down,
sliding on weed-wet stone, and watch her turn
her silver kerf and swing toward shore,
black among black ledges in the glint of waking water,
her drone down to a rumble, lean bow easing through the shoals.

Standing in bright, cold water I would lift my hands
and woolrough arms that smelled of oak and engine-oil,
reaching over, swung me up, adrip with mud and eelgrass.

'Gene, I think, would back her down and haul
on the steering gear that stood by the port washboards;
she'd dip her slow exhaust to a dark burble
and ease back into deep water.

Then the sacred taste of thermos-coffee (steam in your nose)
as she slid on past the folded coast in the warming
of the day.

                          August 1988
                          for Loie, who lived there too.

The Gift

Words: *Carmina Gadelica*
Music: Gordon Bok

The words were collected and translated from the Gaelic by Alexander Carmichael, and published in his volumes called Carmina Gadelica. Years ago Kate Barnes copied this out and sent it to Jan Harmon, who passed it on to me.

It was sung door to door around Christmas time in the Hebrides. The tune is mine; my cousin Ethelwyn Worden helped me get the kinks out of the harmony, as did Will Brown.

17

Dark Old Waters

I wrote this for the film documentary of the short life of the schooner John F. Leavitt, by the Atlantic Film Company. It's two ways of looking at the birth of a sailing vessel.

Sung with leader and chorus; the chorus lines are in italics.

Don't be think-ing of me *All a-way and a-lone,* On the roll-ing old sea___ *On the for-eign ground.* For___ I laid your keel___ and that's dan-dy for me,___ *On the dark old wa-ters,___* all a-lone. *Where you go, Go well, and a fair wind home.___* (occasionally) *Oh hey, Oh ho, heave an oar and go.___*

©1992 Gordon Bok BMI

Don't be thinking of me,
   All away and alone,
On the rolling old sea,
   On the foreign ground
For I laid your keel, and that's dandy for me,
   On the dark old waters, all alone.
   Where you go, go well,
   And a fair wind home.

Don't be thinking of me on the rolling old sea
For I raised your frame and that's bully for me.

And where will you go with your rail dipping low?
And where you may wander there's none can know.

Don't be thinking of me on the rolling old sea
For I hung your canvas, and sent you to sea

And where will you be when the winter comes nigh?
And where will you be when I'm thinking of thee?

And how stands the wind? Will he come as a friend
And keep you from dangers that lie off the land?

And how stand the stars in the whispering dawn?
May they guide you and bless you and the seas you
   sail on.

Oh hey, oh ho, heave an oar and go.

And where will you bide at the end of your ride,
And who'll sing you songs when I'm not at your side?

Oh hey, oh ho, heave an oar and go.

Captain Dave's Delight

James Stewart SOCAN

Jim Stewart, of Saint John, NB, made this hornpipe for Capt. Dave Kennedy a few years ago. Carol Rohl and I play it on harp and cellamba.

... HARBORING A "GRUDGE"...

Boat of Silver

Words and music by J.B. Goodenough

This is one of the first songs Judy sent me; it feels old as the hills. I took the liberty of using the second verse as a chorus.

I sing it in the key of A.
Spanish guitar

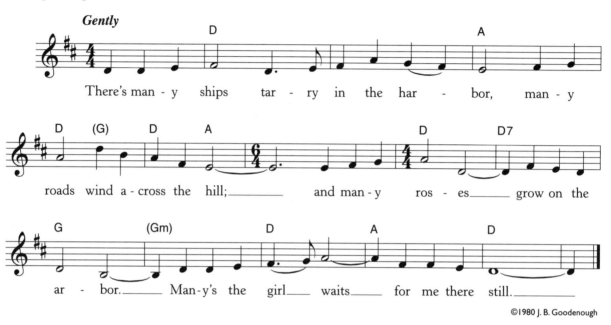

©1980 J. B. Goodenough

There's many ships tarry in the harbor,
Many roads wind across the hill;
And many roses grow on the arbor,
Many's the girl waits for me there still.

Chorus:

For swiftly come all the tides returning,
Swiftly go then and will not stay.
There is no boatman can net the morning,
There is no boatman can net the day.

The fish run deep, oh they run so deeply,
I cannot find them in the seas.
The lonely road winds the hill so steeply,
I'll lay me down now and take my ease.

The rose that blooms blows its petals over,
And the thorns lie upon the bough.
The girls have gone now to a different lover,
They will not linger beside me now.

I will build me a boat of silver,
Steer it with a golden oar,
And I will row out of this sad harbor
And never sail back to this dark shore.

Culebra

One of my last "professional" yacht-delivery jobs was to bring a small ketch back to the States from St. Thomas. Heading into Puerto Rico for radio parts, we spent a good part of the day becalmed off the island of Culebra. This tune is my memory of that day.

Dear Old Vessels
(One for the Taber)

This one's for the schooner Stephen Taber, who's been a "good luck boat" to many good and wily dreamers; she gave many their start in the trade, and they in turn have kept her going. I used to live aboard her sometimes of a winter.

This song was bartered (years back) by Capt. Ken Barnes, who did some lovely ironwork for me. When I complained about the smallness of the bill, he said: Someday you'll write a song for the Taber. He and his wife Capt. Ellen rebuilt her from the shoe up; and, with care, she'll go another century or so.

And to all the others who have built or kept the schooners, who know so well we're all out there together: here's to you.

TABLER

Singer's note:
1 being the higher voices (either gender), 2 being the lower voices (either gender).

1,2   Here's to you, all you dreamers here's to you!

1,2   May the wind come easy o'er your weather rail.

1,2   May the crazy dreams you build always prevail.

1,2   May your friends be ever steady as the tide

1,2   And your eyes and your horizons ever wide
2   May they never fail.

1,2   And to all the dear old vessels, may they sail
2   May they ever sail!

1,2   Long may they sail!

Bay Saint Mary

Nick Apollonio built a laud for me a few years ago. That fall, he and I were driving down the French shore of Nova Scotia after doing a concert together in Wolfboro, watching the sun go down over Cape Saint Mary, tired and happy, heading home.

I was just holding the instrument when it started collecting notes from the land and the water and the people who lived there, like a butterfly net. So I played the notes, and Nick told me to remember them, because they were pretty. So all the way back across the Bay of Fundy he remembered them and played them back to me (he can play and sing anything). So now I have the Bay Saint Mary under October's setting sun, thanks to himself.

There must be a million ways of playing it that I would approve of, as long as the player remembers where it was born. Keep that good Acadian energy, loose and free.

This is one way a guitar would play it, with some alternatives on repeated parts. For two ways of playing it, listen to the cassette of Ann Muir (hammered dulcimer) and myself on the laud on Jeremy Brown and Jeannie Teal.

28

Against the Moon

Words and music by Steven Sellors, Grand Bay NB, Canada

From a Master of the Irreverent comes another heartwarmer and a great song to sing in life's many autumn-like changes, to remind us why we hung on this long in the first place. This one, he told me, had little bits and pieces of his friends in it.

I hear the thun-der, its ten-der noise. I'm stand-ing un-der the mov-ing skies. *Chorus* I will not be both-ered by this world when it's gone; will not be both-ered by this world when it's gone.

©1997 Steven Sellors SOCAN

I hear the thunder
Its tender noise
I'm standing under
The moving skies

Chorus: I will not be bothered by
this world when it's gone (x2)

The rain is falling
On fields of stone
A hunger's calling
To beasts of bone

The birds are waking
In time to flee
The winter taking
Their greening tree

The sea is rushing
Away too soon
The tide is pushing
Against the moon

The world is turning
And looking back
At sunset burning
The sky to black

This season's dimming
Is nature's will
The world is brimming
With beauty still

I love the thunder

Archie Take Your Boots Off / Namagati (Northwest Airt)

Two stray tunes of mine. The first was written thinking about Archie Fisher and how he was always flaming around whenever I saw him. It's properly called, "Archie, Take Your Boots Off And Stop Chasing Yourself Around."

"Namagati" (a direction of wind) is a dance from "Song for Vela," which appeared as a guitar duet with John Pearse on *Another Land Made of Water*.

Played on the laud—Archie in an A-G formation and Namagati in a D-C formation. At (2) the top chords are done antiphonally in both recordings of this section.

31

Another Bay

Robin Chotzinoff

Robin, a fine singer and songwriter from Denver, Colorado, sent me this song about her friends back on Long Island, NY. The original white settlers of that area, the "Bonackers" (who lived mostly around Acabonack Creek and Harbor) are more and more hard pressed to make a living in that increasingly crowded and polluted place.

Both Robin and I have apparently changed the words a little over the years. She says she's not fussy about it, but I include here the words she originally sent to me.

12-string in the "D" configuration (Capo 2). Sounds in C. The arrangement on Schooners is mostly Robin's own; the twelve-string is only trying to give the flavor of her strong piano-playing.

Well it wasn't like this last year
It wasn't like this at all,
We were taking the blues and the groupers
From February into the fall
You gotta ask yourself what happened
When you're up against the wall,
It wasn't like this last year
It wasn't like this at all.

Speak, speak Bonac
It's a fair gant end to the bayman's day
Speak, speak Bonac
All the children are moving away.
Has it come down plain?
Is it time to seine on another bay?

And could these be the Lesters? Who used to
    run this town?
When the right whale sang off Ponquogue
They would sail their tall ships down.
There were Lesters in the rigging,
Lesters on the Sound,
Could these old men be the Lesters?
Who used to run this town?

Speak, speak, Bonac . . .

This morning when you went fishing
And I saw you face to face,
I knew as clear as a bell through the fog
That you'd never leave this place.
No more can the hunter in the sky
Give up his fruitless chase,
It's as clear as a bell through the fog at night
When I saw you face to face.
It's as clear as a bell through the fog at night
You'd never leave this place.

Speak,
    speak Bonac . . .

Chall Eilibh

Words by Agnes Mure Mackenzie-Lewis
Music: traditional Barra, arranged by Gordon Bok

Pronounced "Howl eh-lee". This is listed in M. Kennedy-Fraser's book, *Songs of the Hebrides Vol. 1*, as a "coastwise song; words by Agnes Mure Mackenzie, Stornaway, Lewis." The air is from the island of Barra. Kennedy-Fraser arranged it for piano; I hear it more sparsely, with less rhythm.

Twelve-string guitar

Freely

Where are the ships that have sailed the seas out to the set-ting of suns long past? Bro-ken and gone for the tum-bling seas have cov-ered them o-ver from first to last. Nor-o-way snek-ir out o' the north, gal-leys of Ven-ice, tall ships of Spain, with strong men sing-ing have all set forth; and the sea lies bare to the drift-ing rain. Chall ei-libh, ho-ro ei-libh. Chall ei-libh, ho-ro ei-libh. Strong men sing-ing have all set forth; and the sea lies bare to the drift-ing rain. Chall o ro. Chall o ro.

Good Wish

Music by Jan Harmon
Words traditional

Alexander Carmichael collected these words more than a century ago, in Gaelic, from the people of the Scottish Hebrides. This is his translation, which Kate Barnes, Maine's first poet laureate, found in the book "Carmina Gadelica," a book of songs, wishes, laments and prayers. Kate sent it to Jan Harmon, who set it to this tune and these chords. I loved to play cellamba with Jan when she sang it.

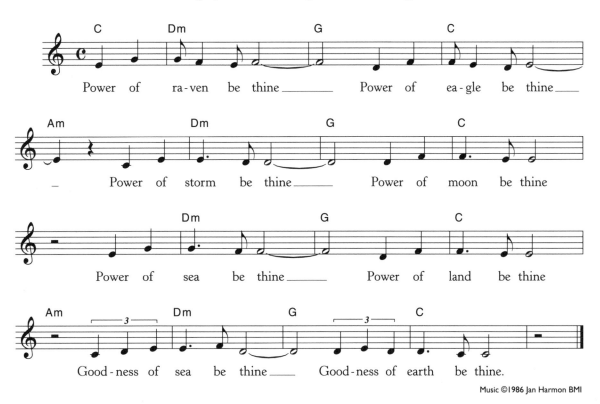

Power of Raven be thine, power of Eagle be thine
Power of storm be thine, power of moon be thine
Power of sea be thine, power of land be thine
Goodness of sea be thine, goodness of earth be thine.

Each day be joyous to thee, no day be grievous to thee
Love of each face be thine, death on pillow be thine
Power of sea be thine, power of land be thine
Power of Raven be thine, power of Eagle be thine.

Power of Raven be thine . . .

Power of sea be thine, power of land be thine
Each day be joyous to thee, no day be grievous to thee
Love of each face be thine, death on pillow be thine
Goodness of sea be thine, goodness of earth be thine.

Power of Raven be thine . . .

Janko (Yanka)

Traditional, Serbian

Working in Philadelphia in the 60s, I met Sara Stepkin Goripow and Nadja Stepkin Bud-schalov, two Khalmyk Mongolian sisters from Serbia, who gave me and taught me many songs in Khalmyk, Russian, Serbian, Tibetan, and even a couple from Germany, where they had lived in the D.P. camps.

They sang hundreds of songs in many styles; Cindy and I sing Yanka the way they did, in what Sara called the "Western style." Once, when I asked them if I should be singing their songs without the ballast of the sound or the people behind me, they said "Better the songs survive with you than they die in purity."

The three Turkish young men honored Yanka, their enemy. They gave him every way out, and his pride wouldn't let him take those ways, and it is his mother who must ask the question.

Played on a 12-string in C and a steel 6-string. I've written these in the key configuration and play them in capo up to that or to a comfort level.

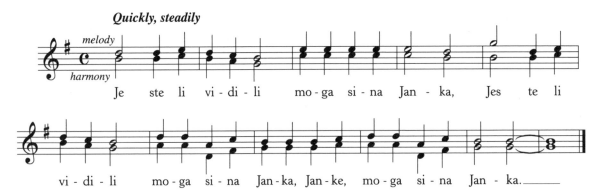

Je ste li vidali moga sine Janka	*"Have you seen my son Yanka?"*
Nismo ga vidali, ali smo čuli glasa	*"No, but we heard his voice . . . "*
Da su ga napali, tri Turčina mlada . . .	*" . . . that he was captured (attacked) by three Turkish young men."*

| Prvi mu kaze "Skoči u vodu, Janko." | *The first one said, "Jump in the water, Yanka."* |
| "Nisam vam zaba, da u vodu skočem" | *"I am not a frog, to jump in the water for you."* |

| Drugi mu kaze: "Kleknaj nam se, Janko." | *The second one said, "Kneel to us, Yanka."* |
| "Nisam vam sluga, da vam se poklanjem." | *"I am not a servant to kneel to you.* |

| Treči mu kaze: "Predaj nam se, Janko." | *The third one said, "Give yourself up, Yanka (We don't want to fight you)"* |
| Nisam vam baba, da vam se predajem." | *"I am not an old woman (coward) to give myself up."* |

Jedan mu kaze: "Bez (i) u goru, Janko."	*One of them said, Okay, go away."*
"Nisam vam jelin, da u gorum skočem."	*"I am not a deer to run away from you."*
	(You see, they didn't want to hurt him. They knew who he was and respected him, even though he was an enemy they were supposed to kill (N.S.)
	"Have you seen my son Yanka?"
	"No, but we heard his voice."

Gordon's Farewell

This is my farewell to a house I sold which had been in my family for four generations. At a "musical" there one night, I walked around outside watching friends make music through the windows and thought: "There's enough music in those timbers by now to sing to future occupants for another hundred years." Bruce Boege thinks he hears a bit of "How High the Moon" in the "A" part (so do I).

37

Harbors of Home

Joan Sprung

My old friend Joan Sprung sent this to me many years ago, and it has told its truth in some odd places where English is spoken. To me it felt like Nova Scotia, but Joan told me she made it in my own waters. You can hear Joan's singing of it on her Folk-Legacy recording; it's also on the TBM recording of the same name.

The sun in the morn-ing used to call me to the day, And the wind from the sea would blow my cares a-way; But I'll nev-er more go down to watch the boats come in the bay, Watch the boats in the har-bors of home.

Trickett, Muir and Bok sing verse two after verse three.

Chorus:
The sun in the morning used to call me to the day,
And the wind from the sea would blow my cares away
But I'll nevermore go down to watch the boats come in the Bay,
Watch the boats in the harbors of home.

Good sailors on the Mary Anne, the finest pledged to me
He went under with the others when the boat went down at sea.
And gone with him are all our dreams of happiness to be
Waiting for us in the harbors of home.

   The sun in the morning . . .

Just like it was yesterday, I hear the church bells toll,
And time it takes forever and the hours slowly roll,
Though they tell me passing days will surely heal a wounded soul
My tears could fill the harbors of home.

   The sun in the morning . . .

The ocean gives us fish and the fish it buys our bread,
Strike a bargain with the devil so that all of us are fed,
But nothing's given free and our bonny boys are dead,
All our young men from the harbors of home.

38   The sun in the morning . . .

Gordon's Fancy

This is a lot easier than it looks. It came from fooling around, wishing there was a fiddler to play with. Look at the slide marks: ♩♩ *That tells you where you strike the first note and just pull off or hammer on that string.*

The chords are never played as such — just kind of scuffed with the thumb or the first finger, and mostly just the bass notes, not the whole chord. On a good, lively Spanish guitar or twelve, I can play it mostly with just downstrokes with my second finger. A thumb or a pick should play this easily. In the old days, we'd call this "Estudio Hammeron & Pulloff." Good practice for that.

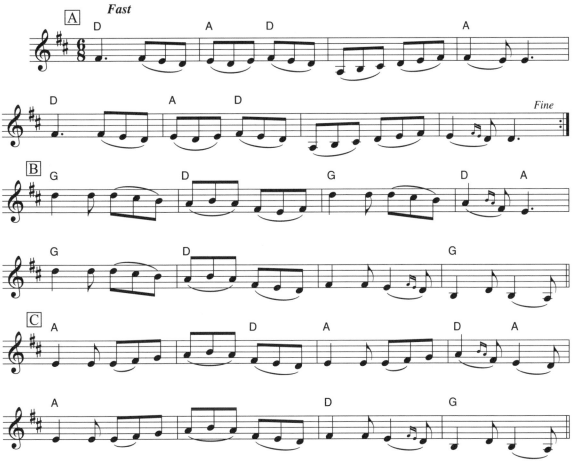

The Wreck of the Schooner Ellen Munn

Traditional Newfoundland

It's not hard to lose an old vessel in skim ice: her seams amidships lie so parallel to the waterline that the ice can reef one of them out so easily that you'd never know it until she started to go out from under you.

Many years ago Doyle's Pharmacy of St. John's, Newfoundland, put out a little book that was half songs, half advertisements. Capt. Jim Sharp loaned it to me because he thought I could read music.

I sing it a capella, somewhere around A.

VARIATIONS:

Well, it happened to be on a Christmas day, 'twas from King's Cove we sailed away,
And we were bound up for Goose Bay, the *Ellen* to repair.
When we left, the wind was down; we headed her up for Newman Sound,
But the tide was strong and we did lose ground, (she) fell off for Little Denier.

The wind came out of the west-southwest and Barrow Harbor we could not fetch;
The gale came blustering up the Reach; 'twas near the close of day.
So to Dark Hole we ran her in and waited there for a half-fair wind,
The twenty-seventh to begin our anchors for to weigh.

Early next morning our hearts were light; we ran her up for the standing-ice,
Thinking that all things were right, as you may understand,
When from below there came a roar: "There's water over the cabin floor!"
The signal of distress did soar for help from off the land.

The men into the hold did make; the women to the pumps did take,
Thinking that we could stop the leak and beach her in a trice.
But still the water came tumbling in; against the flow we could not win,
The skipper's voice rose over the din: "All hands get out on the ice!"

But 'twas our very sad mistake: we found the ice was very weak,
And we had to carry and to take the children to dry ground.
Poor Tommy Holland scratched his head: "For God's sake, Skipper, save me bed!"
Immediately these words were said, the *Ellen* she went down.

Early next morning we bid adieu to bring down Tommy Holland's crew;
We landed them in Plate Cove, too, to walk along the shore.
Repeating often, Tommy did say: "I'll never get caught up in Goose Bay,
And if I get out of her today, I'll trouble her no more!"

Tim Holloway lives on Goose Bay shore, his father and two brothers more,
All hardy men to ply an oar, to the wreck their way did wend:
A pair of boots, a barrel of flour they salvaged in working half an hour,
And leather for Joe Horney for Susanna's boots to mend.

So, now, to close, take this advice: don't ever trust the new-made ice;
She'll hold and squeeze you like a vise, else shave your plank away,
Until at last they're worn so thin, through your seams the sea comes in;
And, when a sea-voyage you begin, don't sail on Christmas Day.

41

The Ledge-End of the Fiddler

Nick Apollonio

Nick says, "I wrote this down as it came to me out of a memory, from when I was quite young, of someone telling me about the origin of the Fiddler's Ledge name. It's a granite obelisk at the entrance to Fox Island Thorofare. Don't know how old it is, but the story goes that a local fiddler who was popular in the community was sailing home under the influence one night and piled up on the ledge before there was a marker there. According to the teller (who probably liked to scare kids with ghost stories) one can still hear him fiddling there on foggy nights. The tune comes from a lumberjack song, 'The Jam on Gerry's Rocks.' "

"The Drunkard mentioned in the song is another ledge to the west of the Fiddler. A pinky is a double-ended type of sailing vessel with an odd stern extension, usually schooner rig, that developed on this coast in the late 1700s."

Gordon says, "I heard a similar story about a foreign vessel that piled up on that particular patch of knobs, but since Nick has made it a proper song, we'll call it history."

12-string guitar (built by Nick Apollonio), capo at the second fret, played in D; sounds in C. These are pretty much Nick's chords.

Come hear my tale, you ma-ri-ners, who sail Pen-ob-scot Bay. You know the gran-ite mon-u-ment that's vis-i-ble by day At the en-trance of the thor-o-fare that feeds North Ha-ven town. It marks the ledge where long a-go young Fid-dl-ing Tom was drowned.

Come hear my tale, you mariners who sail Penobscot Bay.
You know the granite monument that's visible by day
At the entrance of the Thorofare that feeds North Haven town—
It marks the ledge where long ago, young Fiddling Tom was drowned.

Now Tom was a friend to one and all and a fiddler second to none,
And a sailor too, but most of all he loved his jug of rum;
And when the fire was in his bow and the mud was in his eye
Folks would flock from field and farm to hear the fiddler's fingers fly.

Now the Fiddler and Jim Brown set out on the 31st of May
To play the dance in Rockland thirteen miles across the Bay.
With the wind southeast on the sunlit sea their pinky skipped along.
Their hearts were full as the rising moon, and the air was full of song.

Well, they jigged and reeled till the midnight hour and the dance was winding down;
Outside they heard the southwest wind, singing a different sound.
But the boys were full but they must get home, so they up and hoisted sail,
Two drunks alone on the Bay at night in a rising southwest gale.

(Well) the reach was fast to the mid-bay bell and the fog came closing round.
Two miles more, on the starboard side they heard the Drunkard sound.
So the half-tide rock off Stand In Point was all that barred their way
From the homeward run through the Thorofare in the dark before the day.

Well, the bow struck hard and it tossed them out on the seaweed-covered stone.
There they stood in the pounding spray, half-drenched and all alone.
They yelled for help from the nearby Point, they sang and cried and swore.
And the Fiddler bowed one final reel, for he knew he'd sail no more.

All they found in the morning light was the empty case and bow,
And late that year, they built their friend a monument in stone.
Sometimes still on moonlit nights in the early part of June,
You can hear in the fog the sound of the Fiddler playing his lonesome tune.

Long Life to the Moon

Words: Irish (anon.)
Music by Gordon Bok

A short, anonymous toast I found somewhere. (Plenty of room for short songs in the world.)
This is arranged for a male and female duet, the way my wife Carol Rohl and I sing it.

Ogh, Long life to the moon, for a fine no-ble crea-ture, that serves us for

lamp-light each night in the dark. While the sun on-ly shines in the

day, which (by na-ture) needs no light at all, as yez all may re-mark.____

(either)

Rory Dall

Words by Jim Stewart, SOCAN
Music by Gordon Bok

Jim says that quite a few Scottish harp tunes are attributed to Rory Dall (Dall meaning "blind"), whose real name was Roderick Morison (about 1660–1713), who became harper to the MacLeods of Dunvegan (Isle of Skye). Contemporary to him (some think) was an Irish Harper, Rory Dall O'Cathain (O'Keene) who traveled in Scotland in the first part of the 17th century. It's hard to tell which tunes should be attributed to which man.

Was it just last night or long a-go that Ror-y Dall was here? Does an-y-one re-mem-ber the eve-ning or the year? He came in from the dark-ness with shad-ows in his eyes, And the night was full of yearn-ing and the wind was full of sighs. We asked him where he came from, and how far he had to go; he an-swered with-out speak-ing that we sure-ly had to know. He placed his harp be-fore him, in his laugh-ter and his pain, and strings were weep-ing for the world be-fore he left a-gain. Does an-y-one re-mem-ber the_ eve-ning or the year? Was it just last night or long a-go that Ror-y Dall was here?

The Sea Wife

Poem by Rudyard Kipling
Music by Gordon Bok

My father once sang me a song with words by Rudyard Kipling. He had met Kipling (per-haps even learned the song from him) and gave me the impression that Kipling would rather have had his words sung or recited than just read from the printed page. I'm not surprised, then, that so many musicians over the years have set his words to music (most notable, recently, the late Peter Bellamy), as his verses so often seem to be shouting a tune at you. Kipling was born in Bombay, 1865, and died in 1936.

There dwells a wife by the North-ern Gate, And a wealth-y wife is she; She breeds a breed of_ rov - ing men And_ casts them o - ver sea. And_ some are drowned in__ deep wa - ter, And_ some in sight of shore, And_ word goes back to the wea - ry wife And_ ev - er she sends more.

We sing a slightly shortened version, distinctly Americanized, from the version which my stepmother, Stormy, so kindly ferreted out of her collection for me. This is what she found:

There dwells a wife by the Northern gate
And a wealthy wife is she.
She breeds a breed o' roving men
And sends them over the sea.

And some are drowned in deep water
And some in sight of shore,
And the word goes back to the weary wife,
And ever she sends more.

For since the wife had gate or gear
Or Hearth or garth and bield (*)   [shelter]
She willed her sons to the white harvest
And that is a bitter yield.

 She wills her sons to the wet ploughing
To ride the horse of tree.
And syne her sons come back again
Far-spent from out the sea.

Rich are they, in wonders seen
But poor in the goods o' men
For what they have got for the skin of their teeth
They sell for their teeth again.

 And whether they lose the naked skin (**)
Or win their heart's desire
They tell it all to the weary wife
That nods beside the fire.

Her hearth is wide to every wind
That makes the white ash spin
And tide and tide, and tween the tides
Her sons go out and in,

 And out with mirth that do desire
The hazard of trackless ways
And in with content to wait their watch
And warm before the blaze.

And some return by failing light
And some in waking dream,
For she hears the heels of the dripping ghosts
That ride the rough roof beam.

 Home they come from all the ports,
The living and the dead;
The good wife's sons come home again
For her blessings on their head.

*   The version I saw said "field," as we sing it.
** The version I saw said "knife"

Boats of Peter's River

Words and music by Mary Garvey

Mary said: "I wrote [this song] when I went back to Peter's River a few years ago. I had worked on a whale research study there some years ago through the University of Newfoundland, and wanted to see it again. This was after the collapse of the cod fishery in Newfoundland, and fishermen couldn't even go out and catch a few fish for their families. The men were hanging out in the stores in what was probably a state of shock. All the boats were upside down up and down the bay. It is a very beautiful and historic place, and it is just tragic what happened with the loss of the fisheries."

She added, "The bit about shooting their boats is true. A really bad storm came up while I was there and the men did go and shoot their boats to sink them so they would survive the storm."

Mary Garvey is a Pacific Northwest songwriter with more than 50 songs to her credit. She was working on her graduate degree in Newfoundland in 1975-1978 and then returned there in 1995. She currently resides in Vancouver, Washington, and participates in music gatherings up and down the west coast.

Not a boat in Pe-ter's Riv-er, or in all Saint Mar-y's Bay;

Fish-er-men in rub-ber boots are stay-ing home to-day,

Hang-ing out the laun-dry, hang out in the store, The

lit-tle boats of New-found-land are i-dle on the shore.

Refrain The men of Pe-ter's Riv-er are just bare-ly get-ting by, And the

boats of Pe-ter's Riv-er have their bot-toms to the sky.

Not a boat in Peter's River or in all St. Mary's Bay
The fishermen in rubber boots are staying home today,
Hanging out the laundry or hang out in the store,
And The Little Boats of Newfoundland* are idle on the shore.
The men of Peter's River are just barely getting by
And the boats of Peter's River have their bottoms to the sky.

The wives of Peter's River are taking up the slack;
The fisheries has ended and it's never coming back.
Sell a little knitting, set some broody hens;
No sooner does a hard day end, another one begins.
The wives of Peter's river are too strong to sit and cry
    And the boats of Peter's River have their bottoms to the sky.

The boys of Peter's River are as bright as boys can be.
Their eyes are on the highway instead of on the sea.
Where their fathers went before them is not where they must go,
And the fate of Peter's River is not for us to know.
    The boys of Peter's River are too young to wonder why
    And the boats of Peter's River have their bottoms to the sky.

The storms of Peter's River have pounded us for years,
Crashing in the harbour and smashing up the piers.
We've ridden out these storms before by shooting at our boats
But we know this storm is different and we cannot stay afloat.
    There's no nets in Peter's River laying out to dry
    And the boats of Peter's River have their bottoms to the sky.

*   Name of a Newfoundland song

49

Fiddler of Dooney

A poem by W.B. Yeats
Music by Jo Ellen Bosson, BMI
Arrangement: Gordon Bok

Very famous poem by William Butler Yeats. Many people quote it; few have ever had
the guts to write a tune strong enough to carry it. Jo-Ellen Bosson, of Yorktown Heights,
New York, did that. I think she gave it to us when we gathered at Folk-Legacy to create
"Another Land Made of Water." Thank you.

The lower line could be played on flute(s) or fiddle. It is the part I play (an octave down) on the 'cellamba to accompany it.

50

When I play on my fiddle in Dooney,
Folk dance like a wave of the sea;
My cousin is priest in Kilvarnet,
My brother in Mocharabouie.

I passed my brother and cousin:
They read in their books of prayer;
Ah but I, I read in my book of songs
I bought at the Sligo fair.

When we come to the end of time,
To Saint Peter all sitting in state,
He will smile on these three old spirits
But pass me first through the gate.

For the good are always the merry,
Save by an evil chance,
And the merry love the fiddle,
And the merry love to dance.

And when the folks up there spy me,
They will all come and gather 'round me,
Saying, "Here is the fiddler of Dooney,"
And they'll dance like a wave on the sea.

Gordon repeats the last two verses.

Harp Song of the Dane Women

Words by Rudyard Kipling
Music by Gordon Bok

Freely, as spoken

1. What is a wom-an that you'd for-sake her, and the hearth fire, and the home a-cre, to go with the old grey wid-ow mak-er?

2. She has no house to lay a guest in, but one chill bed for all to rest in, that the pale suns and the stray 'bergs nest in.

3. She has no strong, white arms to fold you, but the ten - times finger - ing weed to hold you down in the rocks where the tide has rolled you.

4. Yet, when the signs of sum - mer thick-en, and the ice breaks, and the birch - buds quick-en, year - ly you turn from our side and sick - en.

5. Sick - en a - gain for the blood and the slaugh - ters— you steal a - way to the lap - ping wa - ters, and look to your ship in her win - ter quar - ters.

6. You for - get our mirth, and talk at the ta - bles, the kine in the shed and the horse in the sta - bles, to pitch her sides and go o - ver her ca - bles.

7. Then you ride out where the storm clouds swal - low, the sound of your oar - blades, fall - ing hol - low, is all we have left for the months to fol - low.

8. Ah! What is wom - an that you for - sake her, and the hearth fire, and the home a - cre, to go with the old grey wid - ow mak - er?_____

The Shepherd's Call

Words: Valentine Doyle
Music: Gordon Bok

Valentine sent me this a few years back, and before I knew she had written a tune for it herself, I'd worked this one out for it.

Valentine says, "This is a song for all the creatures of the world, at the moment of their leaving it . . . my version is for a guardian spirit in New England, where all the creatures in it live or have lived, except the bighorn sheep, which I couldn't resist. If your region has a bird or beast I've left out, or you need a verse for a prairie or desert, feel free to add one."

Twelve-string guitar on the second fret: sounds in Gm

Come my beloved ones, come and follow me home,
Come when it's time, your days here are done,
I am the Shepherd, I gather my own,
Leave all you know and follow.

       Follow me down the wide world,
       Follow me home, my children.

Come, oh my forest ones, come and follow me home,
Chipmunk and owl, raccoon and jay,   [Gordon sings White tail and owl]
Come from the cool shadows hid from the day,
Leave your deep forest and follow.

Come, oh my meadow ones, come and follow me home,
Woodchuck and mole, kestrel and quail,
Come from your burrows and grass-winding trails,
Leave your bright meadow and follow.

Come, oh my river ones, come and follow me home,
Muskrat and loon, otter and crane,   [Gordon sings Muskrat and teal]
Come from the high banks, the reeds in the rain,
Leave your brown river and follow.

Come, oh my mountain ones, come and follow me home
Bighorn and bear, cougar and hawk,
Come from the timberline, windy grey rock,
Leave your wild mountain and follow.

Come, oh my ocean ones, come and follow me home,
Petrel and seal, curlew and whale,
Come from the combers in calm and in gale,
Leave your grey ocean and follow.

Come, oh my friends of man, come and follow me home,
Lovebird and cat, plough horse and hound,
Come from the fireside, from farmstead and town,
Leave your warm household and follow.

Come when you know the call, come and follow me home,
Come from the hill, the valley, the sea,
Hunters and hunted ones, gather to me,
Leave fear and hunger and follow.

Loni

Words and music by Jan Harmon

As a little girl, Jan imagined that Half Dome in Yosemite was a hooded hawk. When
night came, it was the hawk taking off her hood, spreading her wings, and flying off
across the valley. In her teens, Jan climbed Mt. Whitney, crossed the John Muir
trail, slept in the Tuolemne meadows, and climbed the face of Half Dome.

When Jan first sang this for me I loved it, but she said the rhythm in the verses
was uncomfortable. I took it for a test drive, and finally tried the verses in 6/4 but left
the chorus in 4/4 as she had it. She liked that, so I've kept it pretty much that way
since then.

She once told me that, trying to recover from a devastating auto accident, she
pictured/remembered climbing Half Dome foot by foot, and that helped her re-
member/heal her own body.

Twelve-string, capo 'way up: played in "G" configuration.

56

High above the John Muir Trail from Whitney toward Star-king
Lon' and I set pace to reach Yosemite that spring.
And like some dream of Gulliver we spied El Capitan
Wild gables, spires and granite walls not shaped by any man.
Night fell like talus from the stone and Loni said to me:
Douse the fire but keep the flame 'til morning warms old Tuolemne.

Chorus:
Douse the fire, but keep the flame
'Til morning warms old Tuolemne.

Black bear roamed the tamarack from Clouds Rest to Cockscomb
Where silent snowmelts filled the steams that burst and thundered down.
And where Tanaya caught the moon Loni said to me:
Douse the fire but keep the flame 'til morning warms old Tuolemne.

Chorus

From dogwood and sequoia stands we climbed the vernal trail
By bigleaf maple shined with mist we scaled the Bridal Veil
And when Half Dome, the hooded hawk, set her shadow free
We doused the fire but kept the flame 'til morning warmed old Tuolemne.

Chorus

Now I know along Cathedral Peak the seasons cloud and clear
And it seems I can't quite count the years since Lon' and I were there
Still when all the darkness falls, it's Loni close to me:
Douse the fire but keep the flame 'til morning warms old Tuolemne.

Chorus

Morag

Music by Gordon Bok
Arranged for harp by Carol Rohl

For Morag Henrickson, Isle of Skye. She was the schoolteacher in Uig when Carol
and I met her—a great singer, full of life. This tune sings to her quieter side.

Carmina Gadelica

Kate Barnes

Back when a group of us were doing my 'folk opera' *The Play of the Lady Odivere,*
Kate Barnes, who later became Maine's Poet Laureate, gave us this. The title is
Latin for Gaelic Songs. I recite this while Carol plays "Morag" on the harp. Kate
and Carol perform together when they can.

Outlands remain: stony lands, moorlands, islands.
The cave in the cliff with the wave running over the floor of it,
Mist, and shapes in the mist; tall stones in the Highlands.
Wind like the bellowing bull and the bruling roar of it—

> But lost is the forest the fleeing princess hurled
> Down with her comb: Middle Earth becomes other-world.

Made things are found, of stone, or bone—or gold;
A few old men tell tales of the race-not-human
And of their beasts: the black, black bull, the bold
Shaggy, small horse, the kind seal—the doe that is woman.

> But the white swan singing before us on the dark water
> Is dying as she sings—and she a god's daughter.

Mussels in the Corner

Traditional Newfoundland

A Newfoundland song I've known since childhood.

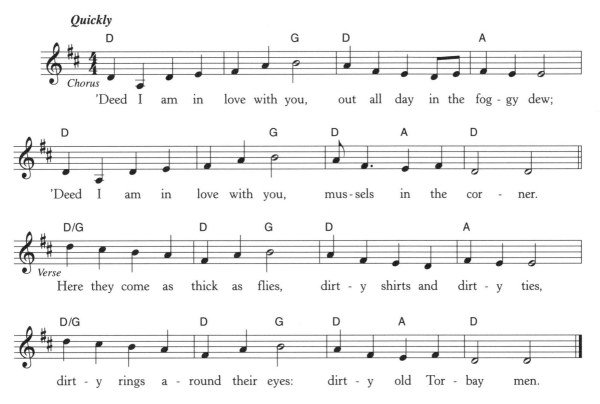

Chorus:
'Deed I am in love with you, out all day in the foggy dew,
'Deed I am in love with you, mussels in the corner.

Here they come as thick as flies, dirty shirts and dirty ties
Dirty rings around their eyes: dirty old Torbay men.

Chorus

I took Jenny to a ball, Jenny couldn't dance at all
Sailed her up 'longside the wall, left her there 'til Sunday.

Chorus

Ask a 'Bayman for a smoke, he will say his pipe is broke.
Ask a 'Bayman for a chew, he will bite it off for you.

Wild Birds

Jan Harmon, BMI

Here's a song from Jan's times in the West, her own unique view of a traveling life. I've wondered, sometimes, if genius might just begin with always seeing the world around you as astonishing, wondrous, heartstopping. And genius she was, from her proliferation of plays, rounds, children's songs, political songs, and choral works to her endless outflowings of visual, tactile arts.

On her handwritten sheet music of 1985, Jan's dedication reads: "For all traveling musicians (who are all wild birds!) . . . . . for Anne Dodson in particular."

Jan and I sang this song quite differently, which she said was OK by her. The music here is from her own transcription.

Twelve-string, capo second or third fret in dropped "D" configuration

Sing freely! See the scenery!

1. Lights flick-er on in a town 'neath the moun-tain where night first comes down like a patch of black sat-in. And the road seems too long be-tween Cas-per and Jack-son when you're tired of trav-el-ing a - lone._____

Chorus

Black-thorn and cot-ton-wood drink up the Mud-dy. Just buck-wheat and sky be-tween Chey-enne and Co-dy. Like a ma-ple wing sown un-der red leaves blown down, it's time to be go-ing back home. 2. You

cross the Wind Riv - er on your way to Big Tim - ber. Peo - ple were

friend - ly, the as - pen is am - ber. Folks sing all the chor - us - es

they can re - mem - ber. And you sleep in a room of your own._____

3.(And)all by the road - side the wild birds fly up out of the

this - tle and in - to the sky! Red birds, Black - birds, They sing as they

fly!_____ Thank heav - en for wild birds! They're all

dressed up in feath - ers, with col - ors out - ra - geous! They soar from this

earth - ly - bound king - dom of ca - ges on del - i - cate wings! So small and cour -

a - geous!____ And it's time to be go - ing back home._____ 4.You can

see the rain com-ing for miles down the prai-rie. Like a great herd of

an - te-lope run-ning like fu-ry! You can stop at a di-ner out-

side Can-yon Fer-ry for cof-fee and a taste of the town._____

Chorus

Black-thorne and Cot-ton-wood drink up the Mud-dy. Just buck-wheat and

sky be-tween Chey-enne and Co-dy. Like a ma-ple wing sown un-der

red leaves blown down, it's time to be go-ing back home._____

Lights flicker on in a town 'neath the mountain
Where night first comes down like a patch of black satin.
And the road seems too long between Casper and Jackson
When you're tired of traveling alone.

    Blackthorn and cottonwood drink up the Muddy,*
    Just buckwheat and sky between Cheyenne and Cody.
    Like a maple wing sown under red leaves blown down . . .
    It's time to be going back home.

You cross the Wind River on your way to Big Timber.
People are friendly; the aspen is amber.
Folks sing all the choruses they can remember,
And you sleep in a room of your own.

    Blackthorn and cottonwood . . .

And all by the roadside the wild birds fly
Up out of the thistle and into the sky!
Red birds, blackbirds… they sing as they fly.
Thank heaven for wild birds!

    They're all dressed up in feathers with colors outrageous;
    They soar from this earthly-bound kingdom of cages
    On delicate wings . . . so small and courageous!
    It's time to be going back home.

    Blackthorn and cottonwood . . .

You can see the rain coming for miles down the prairie
Like a great herd of antelope, running like fury;
And you stop at a diner outside Canyon Ferry
For coffee and a taste of the town.

    Blackthorn and cottonwood . . .

And all by the roadside the wild birds fly
Up out of the thistle and into the sky!
Red birds, blackbirds . . . they sing as they fly.
Thank heaven for wild birds!

    They're all dressed up in feathers with colors outrageous;
    They soar from this earthly-bound kingdom of cages
    On delicate wings, so small and courageous . . .

* The Muddy: The Big Muddy River

Wiscasset Schooners

Lois Lyman

Lois spent part of her childhood in Wiscasset, Maine, where she used to play aboard the hulks of the two schooners there, the *Hesper* and the *Luther Little*. When they began to disintegrate, she wrote this song to keep them and their history a little closer to memory. The vessels were broken up and taken away in the spring of 1998.

Twelve-string guitar, dropped "D" position, capo on at second fret (sounds in C)

Do you re-mem-ber rid-ing home be-fore a dy-ing sum-mer breeze, Your top-sails gleam-ing gold-en, set-ting sun a-mong the trees, And the os-prey wheel-ing slow-ly through the shad-ows by the shore, Where the tower-ing cliffs of gran-ite plunge ten fath-oms deep or more, And the ed-dies swirl and flow_ down be-low._

But the win-ter is up-on you now,_ and time is pass-ing slow, And the tides ebb and flow down be-low._

Do you remember riding home before a dying summer breeze,
Your topsails gleaming golden, setting sun among the trees,
Where the towering cliffs of granite plunge ten fathoms deep or more,
And the eddies swirl and flow down below.

You were solid-built of Douglas fir and oak and yellow pine,
Two hundred feet, sailed by a crew that numbered only nine,
Hauling lumber through your timberports, and dyewood from the south
Running home from Norfolk bringing coal to heat the north
And whatever they could stow down below.

But the winter is upon you now, and time is passing slow
And the tides ebb and flow down below.

You served them well for fifteen years, your canvas all unfurled
When New England sailing ships were found in ports around the world,
But spars gave way to smokestacks, clouds of white to black and grey,
There was nothing left for you to do but waste your time away,
And the rot was spreading slow, down below.

And the winter . . .

From Wiscasset to the China Lakes the Narrow Gauge did run,
To push it northward to Quebec was old Frank Winter's plan -
And schooners were to bring his cargoes in to meet the train,
When he found you idle on the dock, he brought you down to Maine
Where the tides ebb and flow down below.

You know, he tried the best he could, but he just couldn't make it pay
So he ran you both aground, and turned around and walked away;
You've been waiting here for fifty years, but no one set you free,
Now you're broken down and dying, lying open to the sea,
And the tides ebb and flow down below.

And the winter . . .

The people come to stare at you with wonder in their eyes
For times have changed since men knew how to work a ship your size
And the seas you sailed are running black; in time we'll know our loss
It's too late now for you, and is it too late now for us?
Can you teach us what you know before you go?

For the winter . . .

67

Karl Edstrom and the Hesper

Words: Lois Lyman
Tune: Traditional "Swarthfell Rocks"

Years ago, the friends of the Wiscasset schooners were trying to raise funds to
"stabilize" them. They received a letter from Karl, who had sailed in *Hesper*
when they were both young. Someone went to the nursing home to tape his
recollections of those days. It was from this story that Lois made the song and
put it to the tune "The Swarthfell Rocks." I've made a few changes here and
there with Lois's blessing.

My name is Karl Ed-strom, I am eight-y years old, and I
heard that you're trying to save the Hes - - per. I joined her
crew in twen-ty one, for Le Ha-vre we were bound, I was
twen-ty then and I nev-er will for - get_____ her.

©1988 Lois Lyman

Repeating the last two lines of each verse as a chorus is optional.

My name is Karl Edstrom, I am eighty years old,
And I heard that you're trying to save the Hesper—
I joined her crew in '21, for Le Havre we were bound,
I was twenty then and I never will forget her.

She was cloud-white and long, her four masts so lofty
That her topsails seemed to pierce the sky above her,
She was strong and deep and wide, timber ports on either side,
When I looked at her, I thought that she was lovely.

We sailed out of Rockland with a crew of nine men
And her hold just as full as we could pack her.
She was loaded down and slow with logwood and coal,
And her bottom was so foul we could not tack her.

Caleb Haskell was master, the mate was his son,
And a tougher bastard never sailed blue water—
For no matter what we tried, he would not be satisfied
And he drove us all the time we were aboard her.

When we landed in France, the dockside was swarming
With peddlers and ladies so charming—
"Where are the men?" the ladies cried. They could not believe their eyes
That only nine of us had brought her to this landing.

Well, the cook got so drunk that we all ate on shore
And we thought the Old Man would hire another—
But the captain said, "Let him be, for he's sober out to sea—
And he makes a better pie than my mother."

Rolling out to Venezuela, we sang and made music,
Played cribbage, killed rats, and stood our watches.
We arrived on Christmas Day, over New Year's we lay,
Loading goat manure until it reached the hatches.

In Charleston, Carolina they paid off my time,
I said goodbye to my mates, and there I left her.
It's been fifty years for me since I made a life at sea;
Now and then I think of Haskell and the Hesper.

So here's my ten dollars to help you restore her
For it makes me sad that boats like her are gone now,
But it grieves me even more to see her rotting on the shore,
Who rode the waves like a snowy gull in summer.

Woodworker's Litany
(Season to Season)

I love to touch things that give me life and livelihood; I've built and carved in wood, and revered it, since I can remember. When I'm holding something that precious to me, I try to draw back to a quieter, more careful time, tune into the master builders and carpenters who were my childhood heroes, and the younger ones who are walking in their tracks. This little series of questions came together while I was working on the film "Coaster," about the building of the schooner *John F. Leavitt*.

For Malcolm and Lloyd and Gene and Dick and Cecil and Orvil and Nick, and to Havilah too, to whom I owe the ten fingers I so proudly wave.

Twelve string in Am configuration, capo at (perhaps) the second fret, droning on the middle and low D a lot and some on the A . . . the last verse slides into the tune for Langsatel, in C.

Is there no change from season to season,
Save the wearing of sea on stone,
Save the wearing of wind on water,
Save the passing of man alone?

And is there no change from living to dying,
Save the passing from place to time,
Save the passing from form to forming,
Save the passing from dream to dream?

And is there no change from dying to living,
Save the wearing of tool on beam,
From formless to form, from taking to giving,
Dream to question,
Question to answer and dream to dream?

Freely

1. Is there no change from sea-son to sea-son,____
(2.) is there no change from liv-ing to dy-ing,____

Save the wear-ing of sea on stone,____
Save the pass-ing of place to time,____

Save the wear-ing of wind on wa-ter,____
Save the pass-ing from form to form-ing,____

1. Save the pass-ing of man a-lone?____ 2. And ____ 3. And
2. Save the pass-ing from dream to dream.____

is there no change from dy-ing to liv-ing,____

Save the wear-ing of tool on beam From form-less to

form, from tak-ing to giv-ing, Dream to ques-tion,

ques-tion to an-swer and dream____ to dream?____

71

Jericho (Ho-ro, the Wind and Snow)

A toast I made 30 years ago for the schooners we'd been sailing . . . in those days it was mostly human skill and the shipworms holding hands that kept them in one piece.

Some friends and I were singing it one winter night aboard my temporary home, the schooner *Stephen Taber*, when a feisty female friend said, "Bok, for your sake, I hope that's a song about a boat . . ." That time, anyway, the truth set me free. "Jericho" is the name of a bay.

Verse

When she's a tight old sta-ver, then do all ye can to save her,

(Variations...)

(Here's to her lodg-ing knees...)

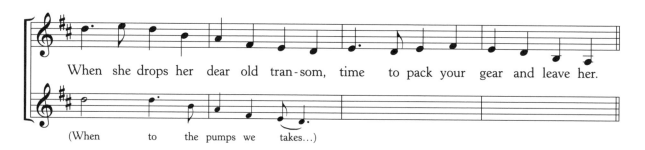

When she drops her dear old tran-som, time to pack your gear and leave her.

(When to the pumps we takes...)

Chorus

Ho - ro, the wind and snow, fly - ing o'er the Jer - i - cho,

When the storm - y winds do blow, swing her off and let her go.

When she's a tight old staver,
Then do all you can to save her
When she drops her dear old transom,
Time to pack your gear and leave her.

Chorus: Ho-ro, the wind and snow
Flying o'er the Jericho
When the stormy winds do blow
Swing her off and let her go.

Here's to her lodging knees
And her bobstays, if you please,
Here's to her trestle trees:
May they never leave her.

When the fog is on the punkin
And you hear the bells a-tunkin',
Then remember Mama's warnin':
Keep her off the rockpiles, darling –

Here's to the dear old lady,
Here's to her paint and putty
Here's to her chain plates, darling:
May they keep her all together.

Keep her full and keep her going,
Never jibe her when it's blowing;
There's no way of knowing
When she's going to tear it, darling.

Don't you go down to the city
Though the women all be pretty:
They'll take your money, darling,
Oh, and they'll reef your mainsail.

So here's to her garboard strakes
And to the water that she makes
When to the pumps we takes
Just to let her know we love her.

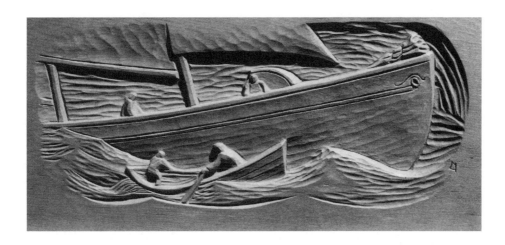

Beaches of Lucannon

Words: Rudyard Kipling
Music: Bob Zentz

Lukannon (Lucannon) was once one of the greatest seal rookeries in the world; it's in the Aleutian Islands. Kipling wrote this early in the 20th century. *Gooverooska* is an old Russian word for kittiwake (a small seabird). Clem Tillion believes that Kipling was thinking of the Pribiloffs when he wrote it. The fur-seal fishery had collapsed by 1911.

Bob Zentz is a delightful musician from Norfolk VA with a huge and fascinating repertoire and many fine songs he's made himself. He's been a real Johnny Appleseed for homemade music for many years.

These are the chords I use; Bob plays it on the banjo, so his chords are a little more subtle than this.

I met my mates in the morn - ing (and oh, but I am old!) Where roar - ing on the ledg - es, the sum - mer ground - swell rolled. I heard them lift the chor - us that drowned the break - ers' song— The beach - es of Lu - kan - non, two mil - lion voic - es strong._____ The song of pleas - ant sta - tions be - side the salt lag - oons, The song of blow - ing squad - rons that shuf - fled down the dunes, The song of mid - night dan - ces that churned the sea to flame,_____ The beach - es of Lu - kan - non, be - fore the seal - ers came._____

I met my mates in the morning (and oh, but I am old!)
Where roaring on the ledges the summer ground-swell rolled.
I heard them lift the chorus that drowned the breakers' song—
The Beaches of Lukannon, two million voices strong.

The song of pleasant stations beside the salt lagoons,
The song of blowing squadrons that shuffled down the dunes—
The song of midnight dances that churned the swell to flame—
The Beaches of Lukannon—before the sealers came!

I met my mates in the morning (I'll never meet them more!).
They came and went in legions that darkened all the shore.
And o'er the foam-flecked offing as far as voice could reach
We hailed the landing-parties and we sang them up the beach.

The Beaches of Lukannon—the winter-wheat so tall,
The dripping crinkled lichens, and the sea-fog drenching all!
The platforms of our playground, all shining smooth and worn!
The beaches of Lukannon—the home where we were born!

I met my mates in the morning, a broken, scattered band,
Men shoot us in,the water and club us on the land,
Men drive us to the Salt House like silly sheep and tame,
And still we sing Lukannon—before the sealers came.

Wheel down, wheel down to Southward—Oh, Gooverooska go!
And tell the Deep Sea Viceroys the story of our woe.
Ere, empty as the sharks-egg the tempest flings ashore,
The Beaches of Lukannon shall know their sons no more!

Blackbird

Words and music by J.B. Goodenough

Another grand song from a fine poet.

Played on the twelve-string in "D" configuration at the second fret (sounds in C).

Black - bird, black - bird, fly - ing late, grease in the pot and ash in the grate, They barred the door and they shut the gate, they got no place for me. Bot - tle's emp - ty and my head is sore, I don't know where I've been be - fore, Lock your gate___ and bar your door, the black - bird's fly - ing free.___

©1983 J. B. Goodenough

76

Blackbird, blackbird, flying late,
Grease in the pot and ash in the grate,
They barred the door and they shut the gate,
They've got no place for me.
My bottle's empty and my head is sore,
I don't know where I've been before.
Bar your gate and shut your door,
the Blackbird's flying free.

Where have I been to? I don't know.
Broken fiddle and crooked bow
Holes in my boots and I'm walking slow
As the last long shadows fall.
The boat I sailed lay down in the tide,
The horse I stole got lame and died.
I don't need a friend; I don't want a bride.
The Blackbird knows it all.

What's this song the Blackbird hears?
I sowed my days and reaped my years,
A basket of sins, and a bucket of tears,
And I can't come in to stay.
My life's a tale that I don't tell,
I did my worst and I did it well,
I never got to heaven, but I stayed out of hell
And still I'm on my way.

Where am I going to sleep tonight?
I can't turn left and I won't turn right
Where the road goes on in the cold moonlight
And the lonely blackbird cries.
I'm going to sleep in a lonely bed
With white and whiter linen spread
A cold grey stone at my foot and head,
And pennies on my eyes.

I'm going to sleep in a lonely bed
With white and whiter linen spread
A cold grey stone at my foot and head,
And pennies on my eyes.

The Ways of Man
(Oh, the days...)

I wrote this song while doing the music for a public television documentary on the maritime history of Maine called "Home to the Sea." It became the theme song, with Ann Mayo Muir singing the full version of the song at the end of the film. If it sounds bitter, remember that the day is late and now the fate of the small fisherman on the Northeast coast looks even darker than it did before. There's no subsidy here for the "little fellow"— only more paperwork.

Written in G; usually played in C or D.

The ways of man are 'pass-ing strange, he buys his free-dom and he counts his change. Then he lets the wind his days ar-range, and he calls the tide his mas-ter.

Chorus

Oh, the days, oh, the days,_ oh, the fine, long sum-mer days. The fish came a-roll-ing in the bays, and he swore he'd nev-er leave me._____

The ways of man are 'passing strange:
He buys his freedom and he counts his change,
Then he lets the wind his days arrange
And he calls the tide his master.

Oh, the days, oh, the days,
Oh, the fine long summer days.
The fish come rolling in the bays
And he swore he'd never leave me.

But the days grow short and the year gets old
And the fish won't stay where the water's cold,
And if they're going to fill the hold
They've got to go offshore to find them.

So they go outside on the raving deep
And they pray the Lord their soul to keep
But the waves will roll them all to sleep
And the tide will be their keeper.

Oh, the tide, oh, the tide,
Oh, you dark and you bitter tide.
If I can't have him by my side,
I guess I have to leave him.

I gave you one, I gave you two:
The best that rotten old boat could do.
You won't be happy till I give you three,
But I'll be damned if you'll get me.

Oh, the tide, oh, the tide,
Oh, you dark and you bitter tide.
If I can't have him by my side,
The water's welcome to him.

Ah, Lord, I know that the day will come
When one less boat comes slogging home.
I don't mind knowing that he'll be the one,
But I can't spend my whole life praying.

I gave you one, I gave you two:
The best that poor old boat could do;
You'll have it all before you're through –
Well, I've got no more to give you.

(repeat first verse)

The Schooner Ellenmore

This is a true story, told to me by an old shipmate. She didn't know that I knew both the people involved, which made it all the sadder. So I changed the location and the schooner's name and made it into a song, to be reminding myself not to be doing the same. *Ellenmore*, by the way, is from the Gaelic words "Eilean Mor"—the big island (I finished the song in Scotland in 1990).

vs. 1, 9, 11, 14

1. The first time I saw El-len-more it was on a south-east wind;

a-gainst the loom of the com-ing storm I saw her top-sail gleam.

Her lines were long and love-ly as she stood in from the bay,

and I stood on the drag-ger's deck and gave my heart a-way.

all other verses

2. She round-ed up and ran her chain her gear was...(etc.)

The first time I saw *Ellenmore*, it was on a southeast wind
Against the loom of the coming storm I saw her topsail gleam,
Her lines were long and lovely as she stood in from the bay
And I stood on the dragger's deck and gave my heart away.

She rounded up and ran her chain, her gear was stowed and furled,
I saw but two upon her deck, an old man and a girl.
As I rowed by they hailed me, and we passed the time of day
And spoke of the wind and the holding ground, and how their schooner lay.

The next day blowing cold and grey, they hailed me once again,
I went on board to drink their tea and talk and watch the rain.
The schooner old and graceful, and built for any weather
And they were kind and gentle folks, the young girl and her father.

I walked the island with the girl, I watched it take her heart;
This land is kind in the summertime, though summer months are short;
The sudden hills, the quiet coves, the meadows in the rain,
The gentle grace of fir and spruce when snow and wind are gone.

Her hair was brown, her hands were brown, her face was brown and wise,
I watched her place her quiet feet and felt her quiet eyes,
For I had been a lonely man with neither laugh nor song
And each year since my Janey died was twelve Novembers long.

Back on board that evening, in the schooner's warm saloon
We spoke of boats and harbors and the islands we had known.
They said they'd searched for years to find a place to spend their days
And here they'd found their paradise—the island and its ways.

The wind was in the mastheads and the seas were hissing by
And oh, the wine and song that night will hold me till I die,
And as I stepped o'er the schooner's rail she took me by the hand
And I told her I would bless the tide that brought her here again.

But oh, the months that followed were a weary weight to bear
For I knew I'd been above myself when the wine was flowing fair
To think she'd ever want a man who made a pauper's wage,
Much less a simple fisherman, and half again her age.

The next time I saw *Ellenmore*, it was Autumn, cold and wet;
She came swinging up the outer bay with just her lowers set,
But I couldn't bear their kindness, nor could I forget my shame,
And I hoped the wine had been so kind they'd not recall my name.

So I swung out past the harbor ledge and drove on down the sound
And hoped they'd never know me from the other boats around,
But as I passed, I saw the girl come out on deck to stand
And across the moving water she lifted up her hand.

The next time I saw *Ellenmore,* it was in the early May
And four long years had hauled their tides since she had passed this way.
I saw the old man on her deck; he sailed her all alone
As past the island's shoulder her threadbare mainsail swung.

He rounded up and ran his chain, his movements slow and spare
And late that day I rowed across, another meal to share.
The boat was old, the man was old, the years had had their way;
He asked me if I liked my life, and I had naught to say.

I asked him of his daughter, but he only shook his head:
"She wed a corporation man; she chose her life," he said,
"She might have had a simple man, her simple love to share.
She saw you go out by the ledge; that broke her heart for fair."

The last time I saw *Ellenmore*, she was standing out to sea,
All plain sail on a Northeast wind, her mainsheet running free.
The old man stood beside her wheel, to me he raised his hand,
And I stood on the dragger's deck and watched the day go down.

Liza Jane

Words: J. B. Connolly
Music: Gordon Bok

At Art Krause's house one winter, I found these words in one of James B.
Connolly's novels, *The Seiners.* I don't know if it is a traditional song or not,
so I attribute it to Connolly.

This vessel had a lot going against her: in some places, painting *any* part
of a vessel blue is horrible bad luck.

Twelve-string in "A" configuration with capo at the second fret; sounds in G.

Now the Li - za Jane with a blue fore-mast and a load of hay come
drift - ing past; *(guitar)* the skip-per stood aft and he said, "How do? We're the
Li - za Jane, now who be you? *(guitar)* Stood on the deck and he
says "How do? We're from Ban - gor, Maine, from where be you?

Oh the *Liza Jane* with a blue foremast
And a load of hay come drifting past.
The skipper stood aft and he says: "How do?
We're the *Liza Jane*, now who be you?"
    Stood by the wheel and he says: "How do,
    We're from Bangor, Maine. From where be you?

Oh the *Liza Jane* left port one day
With a fine fair tide and the day Friday
But the damned old tide set her bow askew
And the *Liza Jane* began to slew.
    Hi diddle di, she'd a' fairly flew
    If she only could sail the other end to.

Oh the *Liza Jane* left port one day
With her hold full of squash and her deck all hay.
Put out from Bath with all sails set—
Two years gone, she's drifting yet.
    Hi diddle di, for a good old craft
    She'd a' sailed very well with her bow on aft.

Now the *Liza Jane* got a new foretruck,
Good stick of wood but it wouldn't stay stuck—
Got a breeze one day from the NNW
Doggone thing come down with the rest:
    Hi diddle di and a breeze from the west
    You'd a' thunk the truck wouldn't stuck with the rest.

Old Fat Boat
(Mattapoisett Harbor Inventory)

I have always felt a little cheated by life that I had never been in a situation where I felt sorry enough for myself that I had to write what Pete Seeger calls a "navel" or "bellybutton" song. (As Kendall Morse would say: what did all those other folksingers have that I couldn't get pounded into shape?)

Well, it finally struck. Years ago I was bringing an old wooden boat from Connecticut to Maine. Ran out of crew about the time the weather started going crook. Threw my back out trying to get an anchor out of the mud. Crippled around Newport for three days in the cold June rain, looking for *any* unfeathered biped who would help me get the old slab a little farther along the coast. No luck. Got blisters on my butt rowing in wet dungarees. Got wet, too.

Got a raving NW wind one day and decided to have a go without any help (had to use the jib-sheet winch to get the anchor off the bottom; always wondered what those noisy round things were for . . .). Slammed out of there with half a bag of sail on and headed her east.

Ended up off Mattapoisett harbor with the weather getting glommy again; decided to get off my feet for the night, so I worked her in there and anchored, got the sails off her. Brownell workboat came out and told me, since it was going to blow Northeast, why didn't I take their mooring . . . over there. Got the anchor up and went over to pick up their mooring. Realized that, with the wind Northeast, I was halfa mile downwind of the town wharf . . . again.

Piled into that ridiculous plastic dog-dish they called a rowboat and pulled ashore in the rain. Called home, went back down to the "rowboat" and, as I was shipping the oars, got a humongous great splinter in the crotch of my hand. Blew downwind back out to the ketch.

Went below, started the leaky stove to get the damp out, got out the hydrogen peroxide, the knife and the oilstone. Looked at the splinter, got out the rum. Properly anesthetized, I was working on the splinter and it occurred to me to wonder what was for supper. Realized it was Saturday night, raining, town was a mile's row upwind and a mile's walk after that . . .

A couple of days later, I found most of this song, along with a list of groceries (existent and non-existent) in the logbook.

P.S. My thanks to Ken Hicks, that outrageous gentle-man from Virginia, who allowed me to rip off a bit of his fine song, "Half the Fun of Going is Getting There."

Played on the twelve-string, with the low string a whole tone down, capo up to sound somewhere between C and D . . .

1.Here I am, man, all a-lone a-gain, an-chored a-way the hell and gone— a-gain, an-oth-er mile— from an-oth-er town,— the wind north-east and the rain com-ing down. Home is the sail-or, home from the sea, he's a home for the mil-dew, a friend to the flea.

Chorus I don't care, man, I'm hap-py. I got an old, fat boat, she's slow but hand-some, hard in the chine and soft in the tran-som, I love her well,— she must love me, but I think it's on - ly for my mon-ey.———

2.No more to-bac-co, no more cheese, I'm sprung in the back and lame in the knees. It's a damn good thing I'm eas-y to please, there ain't noth-ing in town on a Sun-day. *Chorus* I don't care, man, I'm

Here I am, man, all alone again
Anchored away the hell and gone again
Another mile from another town
Wind Northeast and the rain coming down.
Home is the sailor, home from the sea;
A home for the mildew, friend to the flea—
    I don't care, man, I'm happy.
    I got an old fat boat, she's slow but handsome
    Hard in the chine and soft in the transom
    I love her well; she must love me
    But I think it's only for my money.

No more tobacco, no more cheese;
I'm sprung in the back and lame in the knees.
It's a damned good thing I'm easy to please;
There ain't nothing in town on a Sunday.
    I don't care, man, I'm happy . . .

You know, I got milk and I got ice;
I got home-made bread, a little old, but nice.
Everybody puts their cooking hat on
When you tell 'em you're leaving in the morning.
    And I don't mind staying and I don't mind going
    But I'm some damned tired of rowing.

Yes, I got coffee, I got tea,
I got the beans and the beans got me.
I got tuna fish, I got rum,
I got a two-pound splinter in my thumb.
So I'll take my toddy and my vitamin C
And the radio for my company.
Oh, me. I got the hydrogen peroxide blues.
    I don't care, man, I'm happy . . .

Well mercy, mercy, I do declare,
If half the fun of going is the getting there,
Mercy, Percy, you better start rowing,
'Cause the other half of getting there is going.

Sally

Words: J.B. Goodenough
Music: Gordon Bok

Judy sent me this years ago, with a note asking if I'd ever met a person like this. Turns out I had. Marrowbone and Eighty-Eight, she said, are towns near where she grew up in North Carolina. You'll notice that I print the "proper" versions in the text, when I can find them, though my singing version may wander from the truth. "Yellow petticoats" is important. I don't know how they ended up "silken," but I apologize. A poet of Judy's caliber does not confuse things like this.

I usually play this on my twelve in Spanish tuning (EADGBE) in an A configuration with the capo at the second fret. It sounds in G.

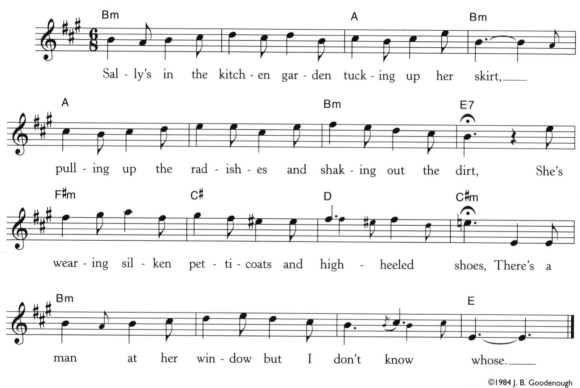

Sally's in the kitchen garden, tucking up her skirt,
Pulling up the radishes, shaking off the dirt,
She's wearing yellow petticoats and high-heeled shoes,
There's a man at her window, but I don't know whose.

She's danced in the sunlight and she's danced by the moon,
Sung every song and whistled every tune.
She's been our lover—and a friend—best we ever had,
But our fine-feathered lady's looking sorry-eyed and sad.

Spring is over, Sally, and the summer's going by;
There's smoke in the air and there's geese in the sky.
And none of us get younger, Sally; some of us get old,
And the rest of us get lonely when the bed gets cold.

Close your shutters, Sally, put the lock upon your door;
No one's coming down the road, no one any more.
There's nothing much to do here, nothing left to say.
So it's off and down the road you go and far, far away.

Sally went to Marrowbone, she went to Eighty-Eight,
Some say she went crooked, some say she went straight,
Some say she's married up, others say she's free,
But I want Sally back again, just looking after me.

Safe

Sleeping in the warm, old coney trees,
fog and rain and miles of silence:
oilskins and an island – all you need –
you find a vast, soft comfort,
safe as churches, and the deep,
aboriginal organ always in your ears.

Oh, I've scuffed the shores for plunder,
dodged the tides and played the winds;
last night I watched the Deer Dance,
and it stunned me.

Now the woods are darker, deep and sere;
now I know how old the gods,
how old the church, how long
I've lived here unaware.

Lily o' the North

This one's for Lily and Charlie Byron of Rosehall, Sutherland, Scotland. He's an artist and she the schoolteacher there; they're both good musicians.

*VARIATION

McKeon's Coming

The story goes that McKeon was a fisherman from Canada. Had a little schooner; ran it with his son or another man. Back during Prohibition, the lucrative trade of smuggling booze into the States attracted many people, and McKeon was one. Unfortunately, he got caught, his schooner was impounded and sold at auction, and he was thrown in jail in Massachusetts. When he got out, years later, his health was ruined, and it took him almost two years to work his way back home.

Twelve-string in "D" configuration, capo at second or third fret.

Now when the wind is bright with the spring and the snow has gone a-

way, the days grow long and the time has come to hoist my sail and

go. And I'll hear no more your dun-geon door nor_ eat your bit-ter

beans; sure-ly it's a long and a hun-gry road 'til Mc-

1. Ke-on's home a-gain. 2. grey seas of Fun-dy. 3. Straits of Can-so.

©1965 Gordon Bok BMI

Now when the wind is bright with the spring and the snow has gone away
The days grow long and the time has come to hoist my sail and go
And I'll hear no more your dungeon door, nor eat your bitter beans
Surely it's a long and a hungry road 'til McKeon's home again.

I'll go down by the Naskeag sound where the tide runs fast and strong
The water's deep and the hills are steep and the nights are cold and long,
And through the rocks of Jericho I'll wind my weary way
And roll her off for Sable, aye, and the grey seas of Fundy.

For the wind is fair and the tide's at the spring and the time has come to go
Hoist my sail on a northern wind and I'll be on my way.
Ah, but there's no one to go with me and there's no one at my side
Surely it's a long and a lonely road for the Straits of Canso.

"Poem" for Jerry Rasmussen

[START POEM]

> O ye who only ever dare
> to sing your own 'material',
> Lissen up!
> How you going to navigate
> without you listen to those
> who MADE the ruddy charts?
>
> And all you brave and humble types
> who sing whatever comes your way,
> Keep listening:
> for so you walk the lay lines
> of all your possible selves.

[END POEM]

BRIGANTIAN THOUGHTS

Hearth and Fire

I made this one Thanksgiving, surrounded by good company, a warm house, and plentiful food; and I could not keep from thinking of friends who, for illness, poverty, distance or death, could not share those things with me.

Anne Dodson and I were arranging this song for our QuasiModal Chorus to sing for a Christmas show and Cindy Kallet said: "Whoa. That's in 4/4, not 3/4." Paul Schaffner said: "Well, I remember it in 3/4." Anne remembered that when I was making the song, I would sing it one day in 3, the next in 4. These are old musical friends with better memories than mine, and it turns out they're all correct: I wrote it down in 4/4 and recorded it shortly after that in 3/4.

A lot of you have made (and sent me) your own verses to it, so we give it to you EXACTLY the way(s) you heard it. As to MY opinion: I definitely prefer whichever rhythm I land in.

Hearth and fire be ours tonight,
And all the wind outside;
Fair the wind and kind on you
Wherever you may bide.

> And I'll be the sun upon your head,
> The wind about your face;
> My love upon the path you tread,
> And upon your wanderings, peace.*

Wine and song be ours tonight,
And all the cold outside;
Peace and warmth be yours tonight
Wherever you may bide.

Hearth and fire be ours tonight,
And the wind in the birches bare;
Oh, that the wind we hear tonight
Would find you well and fair.

*Judy Goodenough loved this song, and sent me the auxiliary verses to it
that eventually became "Turning of the Year." She once asked me why
I had used the word "peace" when the rest of the song seemed to be
speaking more of "grace." I agree. Sing whichever way you like, however, but think about the difference.

Schooner Fred Dunbar

Words (original song) by Amos Hanson, Orland ME
Music by Gordon Bok

A friend sent me these words a few years back. The song was made by Amos Hanson of Orland, Maine, about 1850 or 1860 and became quite popular along the coast. It was collected in North Blue Hill from Mrs. Emery Howard and her son Julian in 1932.

Both Sandy Ives and Dick Swain know the "real" tune and more complete verses, but I didn't think to ask them in time. This is my truncated version, then, with my own tune.

You dar-ling girls of Bag-a-duce who live a-long the shore,___ 'Tis

lit-tle do you think or know what sail-ors do en-dure;___ Or

if you did, you'd treat___ them with more res-pect than be-fore,___ You

nev-er would go with a land-lo-per___ while sail-ors are on shore.___

Music ©1992 Gordon Bok BMI

You darlin' girls of Bagaduce who live along the shore,
'Tis little do you think or know what sailors do endure.
Or if you did, you'd treat them with more respect than before
You never would go with a land-loper while sailors are ashore.

Oh those Penobscot cowboys will tell you girls fine tales
Of all the hardships they endure when they are in the cornfields
They'll feed their hens and punch their pigs and make their mothers roar
While we like jovial-hearted lads go to the Bay Chaleur.

On board of the schooner *Fred Dunbar* well found in fishing gear,
We crowded on our canvas, for Green's Landing we did steer.
When we arrived at anchor the sun was setting low.
'Twas there we shipped young Stinson and Captain Mood Thurlow.

When we arrived at Port Musgrave we hauled in for our salt
We took our little fiddle ashore to have a little waltz.
It was twelve of us when we started, our songs through the woods did roar
When we arrived I was surprised I could not count but four.

On the first day of September broad off Cape Mardeau
We struck a squall from the south southeast which broke her boom in two.
So gallantly she weathered it and it was fine to see
Her walk to the windward with mainsail down bound out for Margaree.

On the last day of September I will remember well
What we poor sailors do endure no tongue can ever tell,
The winds grew strong, the seas grew rough, in torrents fell the rain
I never saw such a night as that and I hope I shan't again.

You darlin' girls of Bagaduce, the time is drawing nigh
When you will see the Stars and Stripes from our main topsail fly.
Get ready, gallant lassies, put on your other gown
For soon you'll see the *Fred Dunbar* come sailing up to town.

And now our voyage is over and we are safe ashore
With our pockets full of greenbacks that we've earned in the Bay Chaleur
So merrily we'll dance and sing as we have done before
And when our money is all spent, we'll plow the old bay for more.

Bok and the Moon

Look, said Bok,
You get out of that tree.
But the moon stayed,
Hanging onto a starboard branch.

You get out of that tree
Or else, said Bok.
Or else what, said the moon.
Never mind, said Bok.

Just do what moon's
Supposed to do, said Bok.
Just do what Bok's
Supposed to do, said moon.

And the moon moved westward
And made no more words.
Look, said Bok, tell me
What Bok's supposed to do.

J.B. Goodenough © 1991

 [shift happens]

You Who Have Found Your Face

I wonder:
Now that you wear a face you knew,
Would you take it back to lands who knew it so
And let those places hold you?

When I see your finding face, it fears me:
It is a face you know, and I do not.
Sometimes I watch it dreaming, cold and still,
Of fabled places, tall and tabled, dry of life
And wonder chills me:
Why should nature
Heal a body to an older shape when the heart
Has grown new eyes, new wings, new fur?

O faceful one, will those old places hold you still?

And we—in this chilled land—so slow
To thaw, so slow to bloom, we've done
A goodly thing: we learned to love
Whatever face you wore here coming. Aye,
And we held fast to demon and to wizard,
Lizard, hound of the dark—and hawk of morning.

Word nor claw nor kiss could loose our holding
Once we knew that it was you we held,
And you a-borning.

Letter to Jan, 1989

Jan Harmon, a person who was constantly re-creating herself, had some
reconstructive surgery to bring her face back more toward her memory of
it before she had a serious accident in her early twenties.

Pearly

This was a very vivid dream that hauled me out of the sack at about 4:00 AM one morning. I wrote it down on a huge piece of wrapping paper and it kept me going right through breakfast.

Like most dreams, it exposes a fellow's neuroses — in this case, authority, crowded places, claustrophobia, and the thought that you might never get-back-home.

Little Red was the name the cop used, and we both knew we were talking about Dave Mallet, though his real name never came up in the dream. At one of our all-too-infrequent meetings, I asked Dave if the name "Little Red" meant anything to him. He said, "How could you know that? That's the name my older brothers used to call me when we were kids." I forgot to ask him if he ever knew a Pearly. . . .

I finally met Pearly, but not until years later, when he was Police Chief in Rockport. A good man, wise and kind, as you'd expect from the song.

I noticed that, as I was writing this, a certain Mallet-style was creeping into it, hence the use of the old traditional tune, "The Blue Skirt Waltz" that I used to play with Capt. Hawkins back on the schooners.

I play this on the open twelve (so it sounds in B flat), but try it in D with a lot of walking bass and the rest of the chords sketched in as they come to hand.

1. Down in the dark and the doom of the cit-y, there's a mon-strous old gath-er-ing hall,____ and a man there mak-ing a wind-y long speech, to the lords and la-dies all.____ 2. Fif-teen thou-sand, twen-ty thou-sand peo-ple, mill-ing and mur-mur-ing there,____ and this ain't the place, says I to my-self, for a fel-low that needs the fresh air.____ 3. So I asked for di-

rec-tions to get me out-side, and I fol-lowed them all for sure;___ and I

end-ed up down, ten floors un-der-ground, and I nev-er saw an ex-it

door.___ 4.The first live soul I saw was a po-lice-man, he was long, he was

lean-ing on a rail;___ I says, I'll get to him be-fore he sees me, and

fer-ries me off to the jail.___ 5.So I ease my-self up on his

star-board quar-ter, I says, Ex-cuse me, your hon-or, for sure,___ but if

you've got a min-ute, and no-thing to do, could you head me out toward the

air?___ 6.Well, he point-ed his fin-ger back o-ver my shoul-der, and

I peered a-way through the gloom,___ and there, sure e-nough, was an ex-it

sign, bright as the crack of doom. ___ 7.Well, I thanked him as nice - ly as

ev - er I knew, and I eased my way toward the door, ___ but he fell in - to

step with me, right a - long side, I could hear his heels on the floor. ___

8.Well he smiled like the sharks out off Lit - tle Green Is - land, he had teeth all

o - ver his face; he says, You know there's folks 'd give an arm and a

leg just to get in - side this place. 9.Oh boy! thinks I, I've got my

foot in it now, I nev - er should have come to this town, ___ and I don't

know what I'm do - in' here now, but I'm sure I'm do - in' it wrong.

10.He says, There's peo - ple trav - el all o - ver the coun - try just to come and

blue - ber - ries,___ black ber - ries,___ tum-bled in - to my hand,___

rose - hips bright with the smell of the night,___ from off of the sum-mer

land.___ 15.He says, lit - tle sis - ter stayed home on the is - land, she vis-its us

now and a - gain,___ brings us all she can pick from the hills and it

sure does taste like home.___ 16.Well, we stood in the dark-ness chomp-ing them

ber - ries, eat - ing them out of our hand,___ and my heart went a -

way to the rocks and the bays and my friends in that lone-some land.___

17.He says, Tell me, speak-ing of our mu - tu - al friend, how that tough lit - tle

fast pick-ing fool___ can find his way through the bram-bles and

rocks of a home-sick Maine man's soul. 18.Ah, but I guess he knows_ when the

days get too long, and the morn - ing comes too soon,_____ there's

no-thing will knock off the edge of your trou-bles like pick-ing an old-time

tune. 19.Well, he stowed the emp-ty bag a - way in his pock - et,

turned on his heel to go,_____ and he says, Well, good luck, and if you

see Lit - tle Red, tell him Pearl - y says____ hel - lo._____

Thumpy

A tune that came out of my work on the film "Coaster" about the building of the schooner *John F. Leavitt*. I developed the theme for some footage of the boatbuilders and sailmakers; it seemed to have the right "gait" for that work. Since I couldn't talk the great ragtime pianist, Glenn Jenks, into playing for that section of the film, I had to imitate his smiling fingers as best I could.

　　P.S. It was Glenn who did the original transcription for me, bless him.

I play this in the usual "dropped D formation" either open or capo 2 depending on the instrument. We've written it as a 6-string tune, ignoring some of the uses of the twelve's higher strings of the pairs. No matter: all these are only sketches—neither you or I should ever limit ourselves to these notes . . . more than once, anyway.

106

107

Turning of the Year

Words by J. B. Goodenough
Music by Gordon Bok

These are words Judy sent me as extra verses to "Hearth and Fire." I thought they needed a tune of their own, so I made this.

I play this in the usual "dropped D" tuning on the Spanish guitar.

Dark the sky and dark the land and dark the run-ning sea, Oh, lay your hand up-on my hand and share the night with me. To friends we had and foes we had and those that held us dear, We raise the glass to lad and lass at turn-ing of the year.

Dark the sky and dark the land and dark the running sea,
Oh, lay your hand upon my hand and share the night with me.

Chorus
> To friends we had and foes we had
> And those who held us dear,
> We raise the glass to lad and lass
> At turning of the year.

Fish for silver, dig for gold: so run the years away
And when we're weary, when we're old, we come back home to stay.

One more road, one more hill, one more stony shore,
One more river to cross until we're going home once more.

So friend or foe, we wish you ease however far you roam,
Who sail the seven salty seas or walk the hills of home.

The Kind Land

Words and music by Gordon Bok

This song came in the waters off my home over a few hard days and nights in August 1998. One night the words came in an unfamiliar language—not too uncommon in my creative drifts—Serinam was the only word of that I kept.

The human history of this land appears to be one of displacement rather than inclusion: this song mourns the passing of people who have had to know the land with an intimacy that most present and future occupiers will never know.

Words in italics are the choruses.

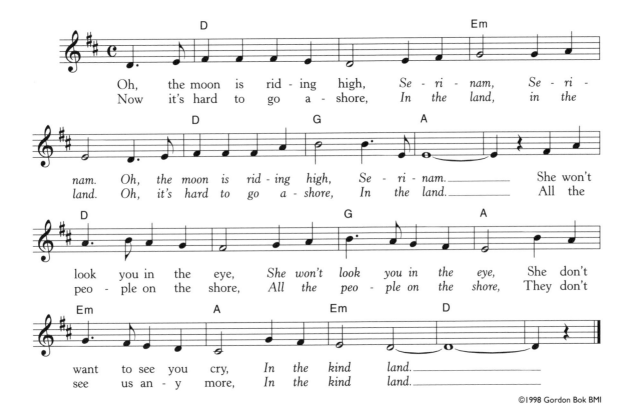

All the people from the town *in the land in the land*
All the people from the town in the land
They don't mean to take you down: *they don't mean to take you down*
They're still looking for the ground *in the kind land*

They don't know the life we keep (*etc.*)
They neither fish nor sow nor reap
And for them the land is cheap

And it's sad to see it so (*etc.*)
But there's one thing it's good to know:
As we come, so will we go

(repeat first verse)

Entrained Water

Making land, one thing you learn,
you bring a long weight with you:
all your tonnage, all your gear
and all your journey—your displacement—
and it's told in moving water.

Try to turn, or dock the boat
with all this shifting round you,
you're in trouble: it will move you
where you have no wish to go.

Know it's there, then, know its weight,
know that you have set it into motion;
feel it, wait it out and let it pass.
Then you're in clear water
and your movements are your own.

Oh—and coming home (the boat secured)
remember: no one here has sailed with you.
So there's another weight of water
wanting letting go.

©1991 Gordon Bok

Jan Harmon

Jan Harmon was born in Saginaw, MI on May 8, 1940, and lived in many places, from Southern California to Maine.

She was a published poet, a writer of short stories and biographical non-fiction, as well as a prolific composer of choral music, topical songs, ballads, rounds, musicals and instrumental pieces.

Jan died from leukemia on July 22, 1993, leaving us a rich heritage.

Jan's publications and recordings include the following:

Clear Horizon (book of rounds)
Hail to the Ox (cassette or book of rounds)
Inca Hoots (cassette)
Moon Tree (songbook)
Rings and Circles (cassette or book of rounds)
Sampler (cassette)
And several short song and story books:
Two Seeds
Pitty the Poor Peccary
Winter and the Rhinoceros
Jimmy Crack Corn
Journal poems

Many other people have recorded Jan's music as well. **So Bravely Dream** is a CD of Jan's music recorded by the QuasiModal Chorus!; it is available from Harmon Publishing or from Timberhead.

For permission and copyright information, contact Scott Prentice at:
Harmon Publishing
P.O. Box 2508
San Rafael, CA 94912
scott@harmonpublishing.com

More information is available at the website:
http://www.harmonpublishing.com/jan/info.htm

© Jan Harmon

J. B. Goodenough

Judy Goodenough was a published poet who wrote under the name J.B. Goodenough (because she found her work more acceptable to publishers if they didn't know she was a woman). She was a tough poet, sharp and clear and fearless. She could see the world as a man or a woman, but mostly as a New Englander, with an acerbic wit. She also wrote tunes and songs, usually in the folk style.

She was born in Kentucky in 1940, lived in North Carolina, settled in Massachusetts, and was transplanted to Pennsylvania.

Judy first wrote to me when we were about 35, about some song or other. She would send songs or "poems looking for tunes" to her favorite folksingers (Ann Muir, Tommy Makem and myself, that I know of, probably more), much to our delight. We had many a happy collaboration, those years.

I visited her when she lived in Carlisle, Massachusetts, and she encouraged me strongly to write more poetry. She was also fearless in her criticism of my stuff: happy to snap my garters when I needed it, and happy to praise, too. She died when we were 50.

She had two books published:

Dower Land
© 1984
ISBN 0-914946-44-7
Cleveland State University Poetry Center
Cleveland State University
Cleveland OH 44115

Milking in November
© 1990
ISBN 0-932662-87-0
St. Andrews Press
St Andrews Presbyterian College
Laurinburg, NC 28352

At her request, I published her last book with the help of her husband, John Goodenough:

Bury the Blackbird Here
© 1991
ISBN 1-879622-01-7
Timberhead
P.O. Box 840
Camden, ME 04843

For permission and copyright information, write to:
John Goodenough
5020 Castleman Street
Pittsburgh PA 15232

Title / Album Locator

Against The Moon	*Dear To Our Island*
All My Sailors	*Schooners*
Another Bay	*Schooners*
Archie / Boots / Namagati	*All Shall Be Well Again* (TBM)
Bay St. Mary	*Jeremy Brown and the Jeannie Teal*
Beaches of Lukannon	*
Blackbird	*A Rogue's Gallery of Songs for 12-String*
Boat of Silver	*Schooners*
Boats of Peter's River	*
Captain Dave's Delight	*Schooners*
Carmina Gadelica	*Gatherings*
Chall Eilibh	*In The Kind Land*
Culebra	*Return to the Land*
Dark Old Waters	*A Water Over Stone*
Dear Old Vessels	*Schooners*
Fiddler of Dooney	*Return to the Land*
Good Wish	*Language of the Heart* (TBM)
Gordon's Fancy	*Jeremy Brown and Jeannie Teal*
Gordon's Farewell	*Gatherings*
Harbors of Home	*Harbors of Home*
Harp Song of the Dane Women	*Schooners*
Hearth and Fire	*A Water over Stone* (TBM)
Janko	*Neighbors* (Kallet, Bok)
Jericho	*Schooners*
Karl Edstrom & the Hesper	*Schooners*
Lily o' the North	*
Liza Jane	*Schooners*
Long Life to the Moon	*Dear To Our Island*
Loni	*So Bravely Dream* (QuasiModal Chorus!)
Matinicus	*All Shall Be Well Again* (TBM)
McKeon's Coming	*A Rogue's Gallery of Songs for 12-String*
Morag	*Gatherings*
Mussels in the Corner	*February Tapes (II: Birds and All)*
Old Fat Boat	*A Rogue's Gallery of Songs for 12-String*
Pearly (Little Red)	*Return to the Land*
Rory Dall	*All Shall Be Well Again* (TBM)
Sally	*Return to the Land*
Schooner Fred Dunbar	*Schooners*
The Bird Rock	*And So Will We Yet* (TBM)
The Gift	*Gatherings*
The Kind Land	*In The Kind Land*
The Ledge-End of the Fiddler	*In The Kind Land*
The Schooner Ellenmore	*Schooners*
The Seawife	*Minneapolis Concert*
The Shepherd's Call	*
The Ways of Man	*The Ways of Man* (TBM)
The Wreck of the Schooner Ellen Munn	*Jeremy Brown and the Jeannie Teal*
Thumpy	*A Rogue's Gallery of Songs for 12-String*
Turning of the Year	*Harbors of Home*
Wild Birds	*And So Will We Yet* (TBM)
Wiscasset Schooners	*Schooners*
Woodworker's Litany	*A Rogue's Gallery of Songs for 12-String*

* not recorded as of publication

Index

Against the Moon, *30*
All My Sailors, *8*
Another Bay, *32*
Archie, Take Your Boots Off, *31*

Bay Saint Mary, *28*
Beaches of Lucannon, *74*
Blackbird, *76*
Boat of Silver, *20*
Boats of Peter's River, *48*
Bok and the Moon, *98*

Captain Dave's Delight, *19*
Carmina Gadelica, *60*
Chall Eilibh, *34*
Culebra, *21*

Dark Old Waters, *18*
Dear Old Vessels, *26*

Entrained Water, *112*

Fiddler of Dooney, *50*

Good Wish, *35*
Gordon's Fancy, *39*
Gordon's Farewell, *37*

Harbors of Home, *38*
Harp Song of the Dane Women, *52*
Hearth and Fire, *94*
Ho-ro, the Wind and Snow, *72*

Janko, *36*
Jericho, *72*

Karl Edstrom and the *Hesper*, *68*

Lily o' the North, *91*
Liza Jane, *82*
Long Life to the Moon, *44*
Loni, *56*

Matinicus, *12*
Mattapoisett Harbor Inventory, *84*
McKeon's Coming, *92*
Morag, *58*
Mussels in the Corner, *61*

Namagati, *31*
Northwest Airt, *31*

Old Fat Boat, *84*
One for the *Taber*, *26*

Pearly, *100*
'Poem' for Jerry Rasmussen, *93*

Rory Dall, *45*

Safe, *90*
Sally, *88*
Schooner *Fred Dunbar*, *96*
Season to Season, *70*
Serinam, *111*
Shipyard Boat, *16*

The Bird Rock *10*
The Gift, *17*
The Kind Land, *111*
The Ledge-End of the Fiddler, *42*
The Schooner *Ellenmore*, *80*
The Sea Wife, *46*
The Shepherd's Call, *54*
The Ways of Man, *78*
The Wreck of the Schooner *Ellen Munn*, *40*
Thumpy, *106*
Turning of the Year, *110*

Wild Birds, *62*
Wiscasset Schooners, *66*
Woodworker's Litany, *70*

Yanka, *36*
You Who Have Found Your Face, *99*